中国风景名胜

Best Scenery and Sights in China

中国民族摄影艺术出版社

图书在版编目（CIP）数据

中国风景名胜／杨茵 旅舜编. ——北京：中国民族摄影艺术出版社，
2003.10
ISBN 7-80069-535-2

Ⅰ.中...　　Ⅱ.旅...　　Ⅲ.①风景区－中国－摄影集
②名胜古迹－中国－摄影集　　Ⅳ.K928.7-64

中国版本图书馆 CIP 数据核字（2003）第 083030 号

策　划：旅　舜
主　编：杨　茵
责任编辑：鲁宝春
执行编辑：王　鹏
摄　影：张肇基　　于云天　　杨　茵　　卞志武　　谭　明
　　　　姜景余　　陈克寅　　陈书帛　　郑　翔　　朱　力
　　　　谷维恒　　陈东林　　吕大千　　龚威健　　王文波
　　　　李　江　　武冀平　　高喜田　　刘思敏　　郭佑民
　　　　杨树田　　张永龄　　赵德春　　吴健骅　　周仁德
　　　　侯宗祥　　向晓阳　　罗大万　　徐　讯　　姜永刚
　　　　张冠嵘　　白　亮　　李伟平　　朱宏宇　　王　毅
　　　　赵鸿生　　任　鲸　　陆　岗　　陆　岩　　刘英杰
　　　　牛永利　　杨　洋　　于　斌　　林　净　　陈克勤
　　　　温锦辉　　邵　焱　　吴江南　　刘启华　　齐　星
　　　　张震光　　吴继学　　杨忠俭　　周沁军　　赵友亮
　　　　胡运铎　　葛　江　　赵　铁　　贺兴云　　李啸平
　　　　周　游　　张永生　　张秋生
电脑制作：刘　彬

《中国风景名胜》

中国民族摄影艺术出版社　　出版

北京华天旅游国际广告公司　　承制

开本：889 毫米 × 1194 毫米　1/16

印张：15　印数：5000

版次：2004 年 2 月第一版第一次印刷

书号：ISBN　7-80069-535-2

销售电话：(010-67018834)

00016000（精）　　00012000（平）

"Best Scenery and Sight in China"

Publisher: China Nationality Art Photograph Publishing House

Produeer: Beijing Huatian International Tourism Advertising Co.

Format: 889mm x 1194mm　1/16

Number of Pages: 240　Printed Quantity: 5000

Printed Order: First Impression & First Edition in February 2004

ISBN 7-80069-535-2

Sales Telephone Number: (86-10-67018834)

00016000 (Hardcover)　　00012000 (Paperback)

C目录
ontents

中 国 概 况

位置和疆域

中华人民共和国位于亚洲大陆东部，太平洋西岸，疆域辽阔，地大物博，历史悠久，山河壮美，像一颗璀璨的明珠，熠熠生辉。

中国陆地面积约960万平方公里，仅次于俄罗斯和加拿大，是世界上第三大国。中国领土北起漠河以北的黑龙江江心，南到南沙群岛南端的曾母暗沙，南北相距约5500公里；东起黑龙江和乌苏里江的汇合处，西到帕米尔高原，东西相距约5200公里。

中国陆地边界长约2.28万公里，有15个邻国：东邻朝鲜，北邻蒙古，东北邻俄罗斯，西北邻哈萨克斯坦，西邻吉尔吉斯斯坦、塔吉克斯坦、阿富汗、巴基斯坦，西南与印度、尼泊尔、锡金和不丹接壤，南与缅甸、老挝、越南相连。东部和东南部与韩国、日本、菲律宾、文莱、马来西亚、印度尼西亚隔海相望。

中国大陆的东部与南部濒临渤海、黄海、东海和南海，海域面积约473万平方公里，海岸线长达1.8万多公里。在辽阔的海域上，分布着5000多座大小岛屿。其中，最大的是台湾岛，面积约3.6万平方公里；其次是海南岛，面积约3.4万平方公里。

地形和河流

中国地形复杂多样，既有巍峨高耸的大山，也有群峰环拥的盆地；既有起伏不平的高原，也有一望无际的平原。其中，山地、丘陵和高原共占全国陆地面积的三分之二。

中国地势西高东低，呈阶梯状分布，向海洋倾斜。

最高一级阶梯是青藏高原，平均海拔4000米以上，被誉为"世界屋脊"。青藏高原上分布着许多高山冰川，其中，喜马拉雅山主峰——珠穆朗玛峰海拔8848米，是世界第一高峰。

第二阶梯由内蒙古高原、黄土高原、云贵高原和塔里木、准噶尔、四川盆地构成，平均海拔1000米至2000米。

第三阶梯平均海拔500米至1000米以下，从大兴安岭、太行山、巫山和雪峰山向东直达海岸。这里自北向南分布着东北平原、华北平原和长江中下游平原。

再向东为中国大陆架浅海区，即第四级阶梯，这里水深大都不足200米。

中国境内的河流，仅流域面积在1000平方公里以上的就有1500多条。中国河流的总长度达22万公里。主要河流多发源于青藏高原，落差很大，因此，中国的水利资源非常丰富。大部分河流自西向东，倾入太平洋。其中，长江，全长6300公里，是中国第一大河，为世界第三长河；黄河，是中国第二大河，全长5464公里，被誉为"中华民族的摇篮"。

气候

中国领土跨越的纬度近50度，大部分地区处于温带，南方部分地区处于热带和亚热带，北部则靠近寒带。各地气候复杂多样。中国气候具有大陆性季风气候显著和气候复杂多样两大特征。冬季盛行偏北风，夏季盛行偏南风，四季分明，雨热同季。冬季，干寒的冬季风从西伯利亚和蒙古高原吹来，由北向南势力逐渐减弱，寒冷而干燥；夏季暖湿气流从海洋上吹来，形成高温多雨的状况。

动物与植物

中国是世界上野生动物种类最多的国家之一，仅脊椎动物就有4400多种，占世界总数的10%以上。大熊猫、金丝猴、华南虎、褐马鸡、丹顶鹤、白鳍豚、扬子鳄等百余种中国特有的珍稀野生动物，闻名于世。

中国也是世界上植物资源最为丰富的国家之一，仅高等植物就有3.2万余种。北半球寒、温、热各带植被的主要植物，在中国几乎都可以看到。木本植物有7000多种，水杉、水松、银杉、杉木、金钱松、台湾杉、福建柏、珙桐、杜仲、喜树等为中国所特有。中国还有食用植物2000余种、药用植物3000多种，以及众多花卉植物。

历史

中国是世界文明发达最早的国家之一。发现于云南元谋的猿人化石"元谋人"，距今约170万年，是中国境内已知最早的原始人类。距今四五十万年前居住在北京周口店一带的"北京人"，能直立行走，能够制造、使用简单的工具，并知道用火，已具备了人的基本特征。

经过漫长的原始社会，约在公元前21世纪，出现了中国历史上第一个朝代溢——夏，开始进入奴隶社会。继夏而兴起的商朝和西周进一步发展了奴隶制度。之后的春秋和战国，被认为是由奴隶社会向封建社会过渡的阶段。

公元前221年，秦始皇建立了中国历史上第一个统一的中央集权的多民族封建国家——秦。此后，经历了汉、三国、晋、南北朝、隋、唐、五代、宋、元、明、清等朝代，直到1840年鸦片战争为止，中国一直处于封建王朝的统治之下。

1840年的鸦片战争后，中国逐渐沦为半殖民半封建社会。

1911年，孙中山领导的资产阶级民主革命——辛亥革命，推翻了清王朝的统治，结束了延续两千多年的封建君主制度，建立了中华民国临时政府。

1949年10月1日，中华人民共和国正式成立。1978年十一届三中全会后，中国实行改革开放政策，实行社会主义市场经济，并逐步确立了一条具有中国特色的社会主义现代化建设道路。

人口和民族

中国是世界上人口最多的国家，根据2000年第五次全国人口普查显示，中国有人口12.95亿，约占世界人口的22%。从20世纪70年代起，中国实行计划生育的基本国策。

中国是一个统一的多民族国家，由土家、土、门巴、水、毛南、乌孜别克、布依、布朗、东乡、仡佬、仫佬、白、汉、达斡尔、回、佤、壮、羌、阿昌、纳西、拉祜、苗、侗、京、柯尔克孜、哈尼、哈萨克、保安、俄罗斯、独龙、怒、珞巴、高山、基诺、鄂伦春、鄂温克、维吾尔、塔吉克、塔塔尔、朝鲜、景颇、傣、傈僳、畲、普米、裕固、蒙古、锡伯、满、瑶、赫哲、撒拉、德昂、黎、藏、彝（按汉字笔数排列）等56个民族组成。其中，汉族人口最多，约占全国总人口的92%。各民族不论人口多少，一律平等。

宗教

中国是一个多宗教的国家，佛教、伊斯兰教、天主教和基督教在中国都有传播；此外，还有中国固有的宗教——道教，以及萨满教、东正教、东巴教等。中国政府实行宗教信仰自由的政策，所有正常的宗教活动受到宪法的保护。

行政

中国现行的行政区划，基本上是省、县、乡三级建制：全国分为省、自治区、直辖市；省、自治区分为自治州、县、自治县、市；县、自治县分为乡、民族乡、镇。直辖市和较大的市分为区、县；自治州分为县、自治县、市。自治区、自治州、自治县都是民族自治地方。特别行政区是直辖于中央政府的地方行政区域。

目前，中国共划分为23个省（即河北、山西、辽宁、吉林、黑龙江、江苏、浙江、安徽、福建、江西、山东、河南、湖北、湖南、广东、海南、四川、贵州、云南、陕西、甘肃、青海和台湾），5个自治区（即内蒙古、广西、西藏、宁夏、新疆），4个直辖市（即北京、上海、天津、重庆）和2个特别行政区（即香港和澳门）。

旅游资源

中国是一个旅游资源大国，有历史悠久的名胜古迹、壮丽的山川和多彩多姿的民族风情。现拥有国家历史文化名城99座、全国重点文物保护单位1268处、国家重点风景名胜区151处。目前，中国已拥有29项世界遗产。

中国是世界著名的文明古国，已有5000多年的文明史。悠久的历史和灿烂文明在中华大地上留下了大量的遗迹。文化遗址、古代建筑和宗教艺术遗迹遍布全国。

中国也是世界上著名的山水风光优美、壮丽的国家之一。有险峻秀美的名山大川，也有风景如画的江南水乡；有千里冰封、万里雪飘的北国风光，也有四季无冬、郁郁葱葱的南国景象；还有千里戈壁、万顷沙海、茫茫草原。中国漫长的海岸线上还分布有许多海滨城市，大连、北戴河、青岛、厦门、三亚、北海等，都是著名的海滨旅游胜地。

China at a Glance

Location and Area

Situated in the eastern part of the Asian Continent and on the western shore of the Pacific, the People's Republic of China is a vast country with abundant resources and products, as well as enchanting natural landscape and brilliant history, like a dazzling pearl.

Covering an area of 9.6 million square kilometers, China is the world's third largest behind Russia and Canada. The territory of China stretches north and south for about 5,500 kilometers from the central line of Heilong River at Mohe Town in Heilongjiang Province to the Tsengmu Reef at the southernmost tip of the Nansha Islands in the South China Sea; and east and west for approximately 5,200 kilometers from the confluence of Heilong and Wushuli rivers to the Pamirs Plateau.

China has international land borders of approximately 22,800 kilometers. The country is bounded by Korea, Mongolia, Russia, Kazakhstan, Kyrgyzstan, Tajikistan, Afghanistan, Pakistan, India, Nepal, Sikkim, Bhutan, Myanmar, Laos and Viet Nam. Across the seas to the east and southeast are the Republic of Korea, Japan, the Philippines, Brunei, Malaysia and Indonesia.

The Chinese mainland is flanked to the east and south by the Bohai, Yellow, East China and South China seas, with a total maritime area of 4.73 million square kilometers and a coastline of 18,000 kilometers. Scatted on the vast Chinese territorial seas are more than 5,000 islands in varying sizes. The largest of these, with an area of about 36,000 square kilometers, is Taiwan, followed by Hainan with an area of 34,000 square kilometers.

Topography and Rivers

China's topography is varied and complicated. The many-splendid land of the country is glorified by far-reaching mountain chains, mountain-rimmed basins, magnificent and undulate highlands, as well as boundless plains. The highlands and mountain regions account for two-thirds of the country's total land mass.

The physical relief of China drops off in a series of escarpments eastward to the ocean. Taking a bird's-eye view of China, the terrain gradually descends like a four-step staircase.

The top of the "staircase" is the Qinghai-Tibet Plateau, which is reputed as the "Roof of the World", with an average height of more than 4,000 meters above sea level.

The second step includes the Inner Mongolia, Loess and Yunnan-Guizhou plateaus, and the Tarim, Junggar and Sichuan basins, with an average elevation of between 1,000 and 2,000 meters.

The third step, 500-1,000 meters in elevation, begins at a line drawn around the Greater Hinggan, Taihang, Wushan and Xuefeng mountain ranges and extends eastward to the coast. Scattered on the area, from north to south, are the Northeast Plain, the North China Plain and the Plain of the Middle and Lower Reaches of the Yangtze.

To the east, the land extends out into the ocean, in a continental shelf, the fourth step of the staircase. The water here is less than 200 meters deep.

China abounds in rivers. More than 1,500 rivers each drain 1,000 square kilometers or larger areas. Major large rivers rise from the Qinghai-Tibet Plateau, and most of the rivers in China flow east and empty into the Pacific Ocean. The Yangtze, 6,300 kilometers in length, is the largest river in China, and the third longest in the world. The 5,464-kilometer-long Yellow River, the second longest river in China, is reputed as one of the "Cradles of the Chinese Civilization".

Climate

The vast territory of China spans nearly 50 latitudinal degrees, and most of it is in the Temperate Zone, with a small part extending south into the Tropical and Subtropical zones and the northernmost tip close to the Frigid Zone. China has a marked continental monsoon climate characterized by great variety. Northerly winds prevail in winter, while southerly winds reign in summer. The four seasons are quite distinct. The rainy season coincides with the hot season. In winters, the dry and cold winter monsoons from Siberia and Mongolia in the north gradually become weak as they reach the southern part of the country, resulting in cold and dry winters and great differences in temperature; while in summers, the warm and moist summer monsoons from the oceans bring abundant rainfall and high temperatures.

Fauna and Flora

China is one of the countries with the greatest diversity of wildlife in the world. There are more than 4,400 species of vertebrates in China, which accounts for more than 10 per cent of the world's total. Wildlife peculiar to China includes such well-known animals as the giant panda, snub-nosed monkey, South China tiger, brown-eared pheasant, white-flag dolphin, Chinese alligator and red-crowned crane, totaling more than 100 species.

China is also one of the countries with the most abundant plant life in the world. There are more than 32,000 species of higher plants, and almost all the major plants that grow in the northern hemisphere's frigid, temperate and tropical zones are represented in China. In addition, there are more than 7,000 species of woody plants, including 2,800-odd tree species. China is also the home to more than 2,000 species of edible plants, 3,000 species of medicinal plants, and a wide variety of flowering plants.

History

China is one of the world's oldest civilizations. "The Yuanmou Man" was China's earliest discovered hominid, who lived approximately 1.7 million years ago. "The Peking Man", lived in Zhoukoudian some five hundred thousand years ago, had the basic characteristics of Homo Sapiens — walking upright, making and using simple tools, and knowing how to make fire.

In the 21th century BC, China saw the end of long years of Primitive Society and the beginning of the Slave Society with the founding of the Xia Dynasty. The Xia was followed by the Shang and Western Zhou dynasties. Then came the Eastern Zhou Dynasty, which comprised the Spring and Autumn and Warring States periods and marking the transition from the Slave Society to Feudal Society.

In 221 BC, Qin Shihuang established China's first centralized, unified, multi-ethnic state — the Qin Dynasty, thereby, ushering Chinese history into feudalism, which lasted for more than 2,000 years and endured in a succession of dynasties of the Han, Tang, Song, Yuan, Ming and Qing, and others, until the Opium War of 1840.

After the Opium War of 1840, China was reduced to a semi-colonial and semi-feudal country.

The Revolution of 1911, a bourgeois-democratic revolution led by Dr. Sun Yat-sen, toppled the rule of the Qing Dynasty, terminating more than two millennia's feudal monarchical system and culminated in the establishment of the provisional government of the Republic of China.

The People's Republic of China was founded on October 1, 1949. After the Third Plenary Session of the 11th Party Central Committee of the Communist Party of China, in transition to a socialist market economic system under the policy of reform and opening up to the outside world, China is, step by step, establishing a road leading to socialist modernization with Chinese characteristics.

Population and Ethnic Groups

The most populous nation in the world, China has a population of 1.295 billion according to the Fifth National Census in 2000, which makes up 22 percent of the world's total. Planned parenthood has been a state policy since the 1970s.

As a multi-racial country, China is home to 56 ethnic peoples. The Hans account for approximately 92 percent of the country's total population. No matter how big or small the population is, all people share equal rights.

Religions

China is a multi-religious country. Buddhism, Islamism, Catholicism Christianity, and China's indigenous Taoism, as well as Shamanism, Eastern Orthodox Christianity and the Naxi people's Dongba religion, have all developed in China. Freedom of belief is a government policy, and normal religious activities are protected by the Constitution.

Administrative Division System

China is currently under a three-level administrative system — provinces, counties, and townships. Firstly, the entire country is divided into provinces, autonomous regions, and municipalities directly under the Central Government. Secondly, a province or an autonomous region is subdivided into prefectures (autonomous prefectures), counties (autonomous counties), and cities. Thirdly, a county or an autonomous county is subdivided into townships, ethnic autonomous townships, and towns. Autonomous regions, autonomous prefectures, and autonomous counties are all autonomous national minority areas. A special administrative region is a local administrative area directly under the Central Government.

At present, China was divided into 23 provinces, 5 autonomous regions, 4 municipalities directly under the Central Government and 2 special administrative regions.

Tourism Resource

China is rich in tourism resources, and has many tourist attractions thanks to its vast territory, spectacular landscapes, venerated history and colorful and varied national customs. There are 99 famous historical and cultural cities, 1,268 key units of cultural relics under the state protection, and 151 state-level major scenic resorts and historical and cultural interest. There are 29 items of World Heritage of the UNESCO in China at present.

A world-famous ancient country of civilization, China boasts a chronicled history of more than 5,000 years. Long history and venerated culture bestowed China a great deal of civilization remains. The country is pockmarked by culture relics, ancient architectures and religion art remains.

Few countries boast such majestic and intriguing landscape as China. The vast country has both the imposing mountains and graceful rivers, and the picturesque watertowns; both the snow-covered scenery in the north, and the winterless view of luxuriant vegetation in the south; as well as vast Gobi, boundless deserts and endless grasslands. China's long and winding coastline is indented by so many fine harbours and beaches, such as Dalian, Beidaihe, Qingdao, Xiamen, Sanya and Beihai, cut out for the joy and relaxation of holidaymakers and vacationers.

北京市
BEIJING MUNICIPALITY

北京市简称京，是中华人民共和国的首都，也是全国政治、经济、文化、交通和对外交流的中心。全市面积约1□68万平方公里，总人口1300多万，有汉□回、满、蒙古等民族。

早在50多万年前，人类的祖先——"北京人"□就生活在周口店地区；3000多年前，北京形成了世界上最早的城市之一；并且，北京有着800多年的建都史。悠久的历史赋予了北京灿烂的历史文化和丰富的文物古迹。众多的宫殿建筑、皇家园林、宗教寺观、名人故居、古塔石刻和宏伟的现代化建筑、人文景观交相辉映，使北京成为中国名胜古迹荟集之地。

北京现有文物3550处，其中，全国重点文物保护单位60处。故宫、长城、周口店北京猿人遗址、天坛、颐和园、十三陵先后被联合国教科文组织列入《世界遗产名录》。其他主要风景名胜有：北海公园□中山公园、劳动人民文化宫、景山、圆明园遗址、孔庙、恭王府、云居寺、潭柘寺、雍和宫、白云观等。

Beijing, abbreviated as *Jing*, the capital of the People's Republic of China, is the nation's political, economic and culture center as well as a hub of transportation and international exchanges. Covering a total area of 16,800 square kilometers, Beijing has a population of 13 million, which embraces Hans, Huis, Manchurians, Mongolians and other ethnic groups.

Beijing enjoys a time-honored history. Some five hundred millennia ago, Zhoukoudian in the southwestern suburbs was already teeming with the activities of Peking Man, the ancestor of the humankind. As a world-renowned ancient cultural city, Beijing's history as a city goes back to 3,000 years ago, and from the mid-12th century, it has served as the nation's capital during different historical periods for nearly 800 years. The venerated history has bestowed splendid culture and rich cultural relics and historical remains on Beijing. Numerous palace complexes, imperial gardens, temples of different religions, former residences of celebrities, ancient pagodas and stone carvings, as well as modernized buildings and new artificial tourist scenes add radiance and beauty to each other, making Beijing a land pockmarking with scenic spots and places of historical and cultural interest.

Currently it exists 3,550 historical monuments and cultural relics in Beijing. Great Wall, Palace Museum, Peking Man Site at Zhoukoudian, Summer Palace, Temple of Heaven and Ming Tombs were inscribed on the World Heritage List by the UNESCO. Other attractions include Beihai, Zhongshan, and Jing-shan parks, Working People's Palace of Culture, Ruins of Yuanmingyuan, Mansion of Prince Gong, Yunju and Tanzhe temples, Yonghegong Lamasery, Baiyun Taoist Temple, and so on.

1 故宫雪景
Palace Museum
after snow

2

长城　东起辽宁省鸭绿江畔，西至甘肃省嘉峪关，绵延7350公里，又称作"万里长城"。长城建造始于公元前7世纪，历时2000多年，城墙大都筑于崇山峻岭之上，墙体随山势起伏回转，气势磅礴，非常壮观。1987年，长城被联合国教科文组织列入《世界遗产名录》。北京地区内的长城长约629公里，是保卫京师的坚固防线，也是万里长城中最富特色、保存最完整的一段。八达岭、居庸关、慕田峪、司马台、古北口等段长城雄、险、秀、奇，各具特色，令人叹为观止。

Great Wall　Starting out in the east on the bank of Yalu River in Liaoning Province, the Great Wall stretches westwards for over 7,350 kilometers to Jiayu Pass in Gansu Province, so it is also called "the Ten Thousand *li* Wall". It took more than two millennia for the Great Wall to be completed, beginning during the 7th century BC. Most parts of the wall were built on the ridges of mountains, looked imposing and magnificent. In 1987, it was inscribed on the World Heritage List by the UNESCO. The section of the Great Wall in Beijing area, lengthening 629 kilometers, is known as a rugged line of defense guarding the capital, as well as the most distinctive and best preserved. Of the wall, the sections of Badaling, Juyong Pass, Mutianyu, Simatai and Gubeikou are distinctively featured by grandness, steepness, beautifulness, and oddness and acclaimed as the acme of perfection.

3

2、3 八达岭长城
Badaling Section of the Great Wall

4 居庸关长城
Juyong Pass of the Great Wall

5 慕田峪长城牛犄角边
Bull's Horn Ridge of Mutianyu Section of
the Great Wall

6 鸟瞰司马台长城
A bird's eye view of Simatai Section of
the Great Wall

7 司马台长城望京楼
Beijing-Watching Tower of Simatai
Section of the Great Wall

8

9

故宫 又称紫禁城，始建于明永乐四年（公元1406年），为明、清两朝帝王的皇宫。总面积达72万平方米，共有殿宇楼阁8704间，是世界上现存规模最大、最完整的古代木结构建筑群。格局分为外朝和内廷。外朝主体建筑为太和殿、中和殿和保和殿。其中，太和殿最为高大辉煌，为朝廷举行盛大典礼时所用，是封建皇权的最高象征。内廷为皇帝处理政务及帝后、嫔妃等居住之处，主要建筑有乾清宫、交泰殿、坤宁宫，以及东、西六宫。故宫，规模壮阔，气势恢宏，布局严整，工艺精湛，是东方建筑艺术精美绝伦的瑰宝。1987年，故宫被联合国教科文组织列入《世界遗产名录》。

The Palace Museum   Also known as the Forbidden City, it is the largest and best-preserved clusters of ancient wooden buildings in the world. It was the imperial palace of the Ming and Qing dynasties. The basic layout was originally built in 1406 (the fourth year of Ming Emperor Yongle's reign). Covering an area of 72 hectares, it has 8,704 halls and rooms. The Palace Museum is divided into two parts: Outer Court and Inner Court. Main buildings of the Outer Court are the Hall of Supreme Harmony, Hall of Complete Harmony, and Hall of Preserving Harmony. The Hall of Supreme Harmony, used for great ceremonial occasions, is the most splendid one, symbolizing the supreme authority of the feudal emperors. The Inner Court was where the emperor managed state affairs, and also the place the empress and imperial concubines lived, main constructions including the Palace of Heavenly Purity, Hall of Union, Palace of Earthly Tranquility, as well as Six East Palaces and Six West Palaces. The state of art design and grand pattern has made it a rarity of exquisite eastern architecture. In 1987, it was inscribed on the World Heritage List by the UNESCO.

8 太和殿
Hall of Supreme Harmony
9 太和殿内景
Interior view of the Hall of Supreme Harmony
10 养心殿东暖阁
The Eastern Chamber of Warmth in the Hall of Mental Cultivation
11 角楼
The Turret of the Palace Museum
12 后宫鸟瞰
The full view of the Inner Court

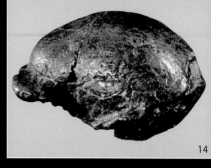

周口店北京猿人遗址　位于房山区周口店龙骨山脚下。1929年，在龙骨山发掘出第一颗完整的"北京猿人"头盖骨化石，震撼了世界。"北京人"在距今五十万年前，曾生活在该地区。这一发现奠定了直立人在人类发展中的地位。1987年，联合国教科文组织将周口店北京猿人遗址列入《世界遗产名录》。

Peking Man Site at Zhoukoudian　The Site of Peking Man, primeval Chinese, is located at the foot of the Dragon Bones Mountains. The discovery of the first complete skullcap of Peking Man (Sinanthropus Pekinensis) in 1929 was earthshaking at the time. The Chinese ape-man, known as the Peking Man, lived some five hundred thousand years ago, in mid-period of Pleistocene Epoch, in the area. The important archaeological find laid the foundation for the Homo erectus in the evolution of mankind. In 1987, UNESCO inscribed the Peking Man Site at Zhoukoudian on the World Heritage List.

13　周口店遗址博物馆
　　The Museum of Zhoukoudian Ruins
14　北京人第一具完整的头盖骨
　　The first complete skull-cap of Peking Man
15　周口店猿人洞
　　The cave of ape man in Zhoukoudian
16　北京猿人复原头像
　　Restored head statue of the Peking Man

17

18

颐和园　坐落在北京西北部，是中国古典园林之首，也是世界著名园林之一。颐和园占地290万平方米，由万寿山和昆明湖组成，其中，水域占全园面积的四分之三。全园分为政治活动区、帝后生活区和风景游览区。颐和园既具有南方园林的景色，又有皇家园林的华丽，在中外园林艺术史上有极高的地位。1998年，颐和园被联合国教科文组织列入《世界遗产名录》。

Summer Palace　Situated in western outskirts of Beijing, the Summer Palace is the typical classical garden in China, and one of the most famous gardens in the world. It consists of the Longevity Hill and the Kunming Lake with a total area of 290 hectares, among which three-fourths is covered by the lake. The whole garden is functionally divided into three sections, namely court reception area, residence area and sightseeing area. Combining the delicacy of private gardens in south China and the elegancy of imperial gardens, the Summer Place has a significant place in the history of landscape gardening. The Summer Palace was inscribed on the World Heritage List in 1998 by the UNESCO.

17　佛香阁
The Tower of Buddhist Fragrance
18　十七孔桥
17-Arch Bridge
19　长廊
The Long Corridor
20　远眺万寿山
Viewing the Longevity Hill from distance

19

20

天坛 位于北京市永定门内，建于明永乐十八年（公元 1420 年），面积约 273 万平方米，是明、清两朝皇帝举行祭天大典的场所，为世界上现存最大的祭天建筑群。1998 年，天坛被联合国教科文组织列入《世界遗产名录》。天坛分为内坛和外坛，主要建筑集中于内坛。内坛的南部为圜丘坛、皇穹宇，北部为祈年殿、皇乾殿；两组建筑，由一条长 360 米的丹陛桥相连。天坛建筑所独具的象征性布局和设计，奇特巧妙，处处体现着古人"天人合一"思想，不仅是中国建筑史上罕见的杰作，也是世界现存古建筑的珍贵遗产。

Temple of Heaven   Originally built in 1420 (the 18th year of Ming Emperor Yongle's reign), the Temple of Heaven is located in south Beijing covering an area of 273 hectares. It functioned as a vast stage for solemn rites performed by emperors of Ming and Qing dynasties to sacrifice to the Heaven, and is the largest existing architectural complex used for worshipping the Heaven in the world. It was inscribed on World Heritage List in 1998 by the UNESCO. The compound is divided into the inner altar and outer altar. The main worshipping buildings are located inside the inner altar: the Circular Mound Altar and Imperial Vault of Heaven in south of the inner altar, while the Hall of Prayer for Good Harvests and Hall of Imperial Zenith in the north. A 360-meter-long Red Stairway Bridge links the two groups of architectures. Unique design and symbolic layout of the Temple of Heaven have embodied ancient Chinese thought of "complete harmony of man and nature". Not only is the Temple of Heaven a scarce masterwork in the history of Chinese architecture, but also a precious heritage of world existing ancient architecture.

21 回音壁
    The Echo Wall

22 圜丘坛
    Circular Mound Altar

23 祈年殿内龙凤藻井
    The Dragon-Phoenix Caisson in the Hall of Prayer for Good Harvests

24 鸟瞰祈年殿
    Overlooking the Hall of Prayer for Good Harvests

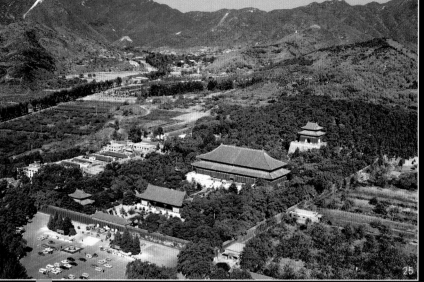

明十三陵□□□位于北京市昌平区，是明朝（公元1368—1□44年）十三位皇帝的陵墓群；此外，还葬有二十三个皇后和一个贵妃。明十三陵是中国现存规模最大、帝后陵寝最多的皇陵建筑群之一。陵区三面环山，中间是个方圆约40平方公里的小盆地，十三座陵墓分布在盆地的东、北、西三面，各以一座山峰为背景，檐牙高啄，宝城连云；陵墓区既是一个整体，各陵又自成格局，各有特色。2003年，被联合国教科文组织列入《世界遗产名录》。

Ming Tombs   Sitting on the south slopes of Jundu Mountain in Changping District, Beijing, the Ming Tombs (also called Shisanling, literally, Thirteen Tombs) are mausoleums of thirteen emperors of the Ming Dynasty (1368-1644). One of the largest and having most emperors and empresses' mausoleums cluster of imperial cemeteries in China, the Ming Tombs are located in a 40-square-kilometer-nearly basin, screened by mountains on three sides. Scattered in and around the basin, each tomb is against a hill. The whole tomb area shows a harmonious unity but distinguished by different characteristics. The UNESCO added the Ming Tombs on the List of World Heritage in 2003.

25 长陵鸟瞰
A bird's eye view of Changling
26 长陵祾恩殿
Ling'en Hall of Changling
27 定陵出土凤冠
Phoenix Crowns unearthed from Dingling
28 定陵地宫
Underground Palace of Dingling

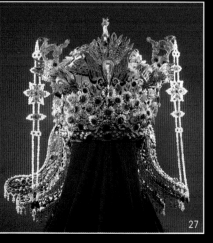

29 天安门
   Tian'anmen
30 中华世纪坛
   Chinese Millennium Altar
31 中央电视塔
   CCTV Tower
32 明城墙遗址公园
   Park of the Ming City Wall Ruins
33 北海公园
   Beihai Park
34 北海公园九龙壁
   Nine-Dragon Wall at Beihai Park

35 古观象台
Ancient Astronomical Observatory
36 陶然亭公园
Taoranting Park
37 圆明园遗址
Ruins of the Yuanmingyuan
38 恭王府
Mansion of Prince Gong
39 香山红叶
Red Leaves on the Fragrant Hill
40 孔庙大成殿内景
Inside the Hall of Great Achievements in
the Confucius Temple

41 雍和宫弥勒佛站像
Buddhist Statue in Yonghegong Lamasary
42 法海寺壁画
Murals of the Fahai Temple
43 卧佛寺铜卧佛
Bronze Reclining Buddha of the Wofo
Temple
44 戒台寺戒坛
Ordination Terrace of the Jietai Temple
45 白云观
Baiyun Taoist Temple
46 潭柘寺帝王树
Imperial Tree of the Tanzhe Temple

天津市
TIANJIN MUNICIPALITY

天津市简称津，位于华北平原东北部，北屏燕山、东临渤海，西北与北京市接壤，是首都的重要门户。天津市是中国四大直辖市之一，总面积1.1万多平方公里，人口约1001万，有汉、回、朝鲜、满、蒙古等民族。

天津市是中国北方最大的工商业港口城市。位于塘沽海河口的天津新港是目前中国最大的人工港，也是以外贸为主的国际港口，与世界150多个国家和地区的港口有着外贸关系。

天津市是中国历史文化名城之一，辖区内名胜古迹众多，又与北京、河北的风景区相毗邻。主要名胜古迹有天后宫、古文化街、蓟县独乐寺、盘山风景区、大沽炮台、黄崖关长城、年画之乡杨柳青、杨村小世界等。

One of China's four municipalities directly under the Central Government, Tianjin is called *Jin* for short. Located in the northeastern part of the Huabei Plain, the city is screened by Yanshan in the north, bordered by the Bohai Sea in the east, and adjacent to Beijing in the northwest, which make it an important gateway to Beijing. With a total area of 11,000 square kilometers, Tianjin has a population of more than 10 million. The inhabitants include the people of Han, Hui, Korea, Manchu, Mongol and other ethnic backgrounds.

Tianjin is the biggest industrial and commercial harbour city of north China. Situated in Tanggu District and Haihe River's entrance, Tianjin New Harbour is the largest man-made harbour present in China, as well as an international trade seaport, which has maintained trade relations with harbours in 150-odd countries and regions.

As one of national famous historical and cultural city, Tianjin is abundant in scenic spots and historical sites, which connect with scenes and sights in Beijing and Hebei, and form a big tourist zone. Major attractions in Tianjin are Tianhou Temple, Ancient Cultural Street, Dule Temple, Panshan Scenic Resort, Dagu Fort, Great Wall at Huangya Pass, Yangliuqing, a home to New Year Pictures and Yangcun Amusement Park.

1 古文化街
Ancient Cultural Street

2 黄崖关长城　位于蓟县北30公里处，始建于北齐天保七年（公元556年），明隆庆年间（公元1567—1572年）重修，是长城沿线著名的关隘之一。城墙建在陡峭山脊之上，敌楼墩台、边城掩体，设施完备。因此段长城地处北京、天津、河北交界之处，是扼守长城东部的重要关口，故有"京东雁门关"之誉。

Huangya Pass　Standing 30 kilometers north of Jixian County, the Huangya Pass was one of the most famous passes of the Great Wall. It was originally built in 556, or the seventh year of the Tianbao reign of the Northern Qi Dynasty, and rebuilt during the Longqing reign (1567-1572) of the Ming Dynasty. This section of the Great Wall with its watchtowers, battlements and barracks and moated defense works, is built on sharp mountain ridges. Located at the juncture of Beijing, Tianjin and Hebei Province, the Huangya Pass is a strategic pass holding access to the eastern part of the Great Wall, and is reputed as "the Yanmen Pass to the east of Beijing".

3 盘山风景名胜区 位于蓟县西北12公里处，因雄踞北京之东，故被誉为"京东第一山"。景区面积106平方公里，海拔864米，有五峰、八石及72座寺庙等名胜。

Panshan Scenic Resort 12 kilometers northwest of Jixian County, the Panshan Mountain was reputed as "No. 1 Mountain to the East of Beijing" for its location. The scenic resort covers an area of 106 square kilometers and has an elevation of 864 meters above sea level. Major attractions of Panshan Mountain are five peaks, eight rocks and 72 Buddhist monasteries and Taoist temples, and so on.

4、5 独乐寺 位于蓟县城西，始建于唐朝。寺院由山门、观音阁及左右配殿组成。观音阁通高23米，虽经过多次地震，至今仍岿然不动，是中国现存最早的木结构楼阁建筑之一。阁内供奉十一面观音塑像，高达16米，为辽代雕塑艺术珍品。

Dule Temple Located in Jixian County, the Dule Temple, or the Solitary Joy Temple, was first constructed during the Tang Dynasty (618-907). The temple consists of a frontal archway, the Guanyin (Avalokitesvara) Pavilion, and its secondary halls. 23 meters in height, the Guanyin Pavilion stands formidable despite many earthquakes, and is one of the oldest wooden pavilion-style structures in China. Inside the pavilion is a 16-meter-high statue of Avalokitesvara with eleven faces, a rare treasure among sculptures following the style of the Liao Dynasty (916-1125).

4

5

6 水上公园
Over-Water Park

7、8 杨柳青年画　因产于天津西南杨柳青而得名，是中国著名的年画品种之一。年画用木板刻印，题材多样，主要有仕女、娃娃、佛像、民间故事等。

Yangliuqing New Year Picture　It is one of most famous New Year Pictures in China, which is made in Yangliuqing, located in the western suburb of Tianjin Municipality and hence the name. Usually made by the block-printing method, the pictures are characterized by simple, clear lines, brilliant colors and scenes of prosperity. The themes expressed in New Year Pictures cover a wide range, such as beauties, children, Buddhist images, folk tales, and so on.

河北省
HEBEI PROVINCE

河北省简称冀，位于华北平原北部，东临渤海。春秋战国时期地属燕国和赵国，故有"燕赵"之称；元、明、清三朝定都北京后，河北成为拱卫京师的畿辅之地，又称为"京畿"。全省面积19万多平方公里，人口6744万，有汉、回、满、蒙古、朝鲜等民族。省会石家庄市。

河北省是中国著名的文物大省，名胜古迹遍布全省各地。现有世界遗产3处，历史文化名城5座，省级以上文物保护单位670余处。主要文物古迹有承德避暑山庄及外八庙，清东陵与清西陵，金山岭、山海关、老龙头等段长城，正定隆兴寺，邯郸丛台，赵县安济桥，沧州铁狮子，响堂山石窟等。

河北省地貌、地形齐全，自然风光秀美，有中国十大风景名胜区2处，国家级风景名胜区5处，国家级森林公园9处。秦皇岛北戴河海滨、"华北明珠"白洋淀风景区、坝上草原、苍岩山、天桂山、野三坡风景区等均为旅游胜地。

Hebei Province, abbreviated as *Ji*, is located in the northern part of Huabei (North China) Plain, facing the Bohai Sea in the east. It is also called "Yanzhao" because it used to be the territory of the Yan and the Zhao states during the periods of Spring and Autumn and Warring States. During the Yuan, Ming and Qing dynasties, Hebei became most important because Beijing was chose to be the capital, and was known as the environs of the capital. Covering an area of more than 190,000 square kilometers, the province has a population of 67.44 million of Han, Hui, Manchu, Mongolian, Korean and other ethnic backgrounds. The provincial capital is Shijiazhuang.

As a famous province of cultural relics in China, Hebei has numerous historical sites and scenic spots pockmarking throughout its whole territory. There are three world heritage sites, five national famous historical and cultural cities, and more than 670 sites of historical and cultural interest which are under key protection at or above the provincial level. Major cultural relics and historical remains include the Mountain Resort and its outlying imperial temples in Chengde, Eastern and Western Imperial Tombs of the Qing Dynasty, the Great Wall at Jinshanling, Shanhaiguan and Laolongtou sections, Longxing Temple in Zhengding, Congtai Terrace in Handan, Anji Bridge in Zhaoxian County, Iron Lion in Cangzhou and Xiangtangshan Mountain Grottoes in Handan.

Hebei possesses multiplex landscapes such as seashores, plains, lakes, mountains and plateau, as well as most diversified natural scenery. There are two national top ten scenic spots, five national scenic resorts and nine national forest parks in the province. Major tourist attractions are Beidaihe Beach in Qinhuangdao, Baiyangdian scenic resort, known as "the Pearl of North China", Bashang Grassland, Cangyan Mountain, Tiangui Mountain and Yesanpo Scenic Area.

1 承德避暑山庄
Chengde Mountain Resort

承德避暑山庄　坐落于承德市，是中国现存最大的皇家园林，为清朝皇帝避暑行宫。山庄占地面积564万平方米，始建于清康熙四十二年（公元1703年），历时长达90年。园内建有各种风格的建筑130余处，建筑面积10万多平方米，兼有南方园林的精致和皇家园林的华丽。1994年，避暑山庄被联合国教科文组织列入《世界遗产名录》。

Chengde Mountain Resort　It was the summer residence of the Qing Dynasty (1644—1911) imperial family. Extending over 5.64 million square meters in the urban area of Chengde, it is the largest imperial park extant in China. The construction of the resort began in 1703, or the 42nd year of the Qing Emperor Kangxi's reign, and last for 90 years. Scattered across the Mountain Resort are some 130 groups of structures built in different styles and totaling about 100,000 square meters in floor space. The Mountain Resort combines the delicacy of private gardens in south China and the elegancy of imperial gardens in north China. It was inscribed on the World Heritage List by UNESCO in 1994.

3

2 避暑山庄正门
Front Entrance of the Chengde
Mountain Resort
3 山庄晨雾
The Mountain Resort in morning mist
4 南山积雪亭
Pavilion of Southern Mountains
under Snow
5 澹泊敬诚殿内景
Interior of the Hall of
Simplicity and Mist Sincerity

4

5

承德避暑山庄周围寺庙　在承德避暑山庄东面和北面山麓，坐落着一组特色各异的寺庙，雄伟壮观，金碧辉煌，似众星捧月，与避暑山庄交相辉映，具有汉、藏、蒙等民族建筑风格。1994年，他们与承德避暑山庄一起被联合国教科文组织列入《世界遗产名录》。

The Mountain Resort's Outlying Temples Located northeast of the Mountain Resort is a group of temple buildings in the styles of different ethnic groups of Han, Tibetan and Mongolian. The Temples are magnificent and spectacular, and they set off the Mountain Resort as stars set off the moon. Together with the Mountain Resort, they were inscribed on the World Heritage List by UNESCO in 1994.

6　普乐寺　建于清乾隆三十一年（公元1766年），坐东朝西，占地面积约2.4万平方米。主殿旭光阁，高23米，直径21.68米，为仿照北京天坛祈年殿而建。

Pulesi (Temple of Universal Joy)　The temple was built in 1766 and covers an area of 24,000 square meters, facing west. Xuguang-ge (Pavilion of the Rising Sun), its principle structure, 23 meters in height and 21.68 meters in diameter, is a replica of the Hall of Prayer for Good Harvests in Beijing's Temple of Heaven.

7　普陀宗乘之庙
　Temple of the Potarake Doctrine
8　普宁寺
　Temple of Universal Peace

9 山海关　位于秦皇岛市东北15公里处，北依燕山，南濒渤海，因此得名。山海关关城建于明洪武十四年（公元1381年），由名将徐达督建，是明长城东部最重要的关口。关城辟有镇东、迎恩、望洋、威远四座城门，城墙高达14米，砖石包砌，威武壮观，是明长城东部最为重要的关口，自古便有"天下第一关"之誉。

Shanhai Pass   Situated in the 15 kilometers northeast of the city of Qinghuangdao, it is so-called for its location between the Yanshan Mountain and the Bohai Sea. Built in 1381 (the 14th year of the Ming Emperor Hongwu's reign) by Xu Da, the famous Ming-Dynasty general, the pass is the most important one in the eastern part of the Great Wall. The pass has four gates, named "Zhendong", "Ying'en", "Wangyang" and "Weiyuan" respectively. The wall stands 14 meters in height and is lined with bricks and stones. The gate-tower looks majestic, and has been extolled as "Number One Pass Under Heaven" since ancient times.

10 老龙头
Laolongtou section of the Great Wall

11 金山岭长城　位于河北省滦平县与北京市密云县交界处，南距北京120公里，因部分长城建筑于金山之上，故名。现存城墙多为明隆庆四年（公元1570年）修建。金山岭长城气势雄伟，视野开阔，结构复杂，地势险要；每隔60米至200米，就建有一座敌楼，在大约30公里的城墙上建有敌楼158座之多。

Jinshanling Section of the Great Wall　It is situated 120 kilometers from Beijing, where the boundaries of Miyun County of Beijing and Luanping County of Hebei Province cross. Its name derived from the Jinshan Mountains. Most parts of the wall of the section existing now were built in 1570 (the fourth year of Ming Emperor Longqing's reign). The Jinshanling section of the Great Wall towers magnificently over a broad

13

12

14

15

vista of the surroundings. The buildings come in diverse forms and watchtowers are clustered in places of strategic importance at intervals of 60 and 200 meters. There are 158 watchtowers totally built on about 30 kilometers walls.

12 金山岭雪景
Jinshanling after snow

13 金山岭大金山楼
Greater Jinshan Tower

14 金山岭之夏
Jinshanling in summer

15 鹿皮关长城
Lupiguan section of the Great Wall

清东陵　位于遵化市西北部的昌瑞山南麓，是清朝的皇家陵园，占地面积48平方公里，规模宏大，体系完整。陵区内共建帝陵5座，葬有顺治、康熙、乾隆、咸丰、同治等五位皇帝；还埋葬有孝庄文皇后、慈禧太后等15位皇后以及100多位嫔妃。2000年，清东陵被联合国教科文组织列入《世界遗产名录》。

Eastern Tombs of the Qing Dynasty　Situated on the south slope of Mount Changrui in Zunhua, it is an imperial graveyard of the Qing Dynasty. With an area of 48 square kilometers, it is one of the largest and most complete group imperial tombs in China. Five emperors — Shunzhi, Kangxi, Qianlong, Xianfeng and Tongzhi — and 15 empresses such as Empress Xiaozhuang and Empress Dowager Cixi were buried here. There are also tombs for over 100 imperial concubines. In 2000, UNESCO inscribed it on the World Heritage List.

18

19

16 定陵（咸丰皇帝陵）
Dingling (Tomb of Emperor Xianfeng)

17 定东陵（慈禧、慈安陵）
Dingdongling (Tombs of Empress
Dowagers Cixi and Ci'an)

18 孝陵（顺治皇帝陵）
Xiaoling (Tomb of Emperor Shunzhi)

19 东陵雪霁
Eastern Tombs after snow

20 远眺东陵
A bird's eye view of the Eastern Tombs of
the Qing Dynasty

20

河北

清西陵　位于易县，始建于清雍正八年（公元1730年），完工于1915年。陵区面积800多平方公里，共葬有4位皇帝、3位皇后以及69位皇子、公主和嫔妃，是中国清朝陵寝建筑艺术的代表作品。2000年，清西陵被联合国教科文组织列入《世界遗产名录》。

Western Tombs of the Qing Dynasty　Located in Yi County, the Western Tombs are eternal sleeping chambers for four emperors, three empresses and 69 princes, princesses and imperial concubines of the dynasty. The entire area of some 800 square kilometers is walled on all sides by green hills. Construction of the tombs began in 1730 (the eighth year of Qing Emperor Yongzhen's reign) and completed after 185 years in 1915. The tombs are outstanding representatives of Qing mausoleum-building art, and in 2000, they were inscribed on the World Heritage List by UNESCO.

21 崇陵（光绪皇帝陵）地宫
Underground Palace of Chongling
(Tomb of Emperor Guangxu)
22 清西陵雕刻
Bronze Carving
23 清西陵牌坊
Stone archways of the Western Tombs of the Qing Dynasty

21

23

24

24 安济桥 又名赵州桥，位于赵县城南的交河上，是中国最早的石拱桥。该桥建于隋朝年间（公元581－618年），由著名工匠李春设计建造。安济桥全长 50.82米，宽9.6米，跨度37米。桥梁望柱栏板石雕，雕刻精细，是隋代石雕艺术的杰作。

Anji Bridge   Also called Zhaozhou Bridge, it is located in Zhaoxian County. The bridge spans the Jiao River, and has done for 1,300 years during the Sui Dynasty (581 — 618AD) by Li Chun, a famous artisan then. It is 50.82 meters long, 9.6 meters wide, with a span of 37 meters, and is believed as the oldest stone-arch bridge in China. The balustrades and railing boards are carved with dragons and mythical creatures, which reflect excellent stone-carving skills of the Sui Dynasty.

25 邯郸丛台
Congtai Terrace, Handan
26 正定隆兴寺大铜佛
Bronze Buddha in Longxing Temple, Zhengding

25

26

27 白洋淀风景区
Baiyangdian Scenic Area
28 正定隆兴寺倒坐观音
Guanyin Bodhisattva in Longxing
Temple, Zhengding
29 坝上草原
Grassland on the Fengning Tableland

中国风景名胜

31

32

31–33 北戴河　位于秦皇岛市西南15公里处。北依联峰山，东起鹰角石，西至戴河口，全长10公里，是中国著名的避暑胜地。海滨景色优美，沙软滩平，海水清澈，山上松柏葱郁，怪石、幽径、曲桥、亭塔、错落其间，相映成趣。鹰角石鸽子窝是观日出的旅游胜地。

Beidaihe Beach Resort　　15 kilometers southwest of Qinhuangdao City, the Beidaihe Beach is a famous scenic summer resort. It stretches 10 kilometers east to west from the Yingjiao Rock to the mouth of Daihe River. Its charm lies mostly in the soft sands, gentle beach and clear seawater. The environment around Beidaihe is also beautiful. Mt. Lianfeng, backing onto the beach, has two peaks covered by abundant green pines and cypresses. Lush vegetation, strange stones, decorated pavilions, secluded paths, ancient pagodas and winding bridges cover the mountain and make it unique and appealing. "The Dove Nest" is one of popular attractions, where visitors can enjoy watching the sunrising and powerfully energetic ocean.

33

山西省
SHANXI PROVINCE

山西省简称晋，位于华北平原西侧，与河北、河南、内蒙古、陕西等省、自治区相邻。因地处太行山以西而得名。全省面积15万多平方公里，人口3297万，主要有汉、回、满、蒙古等民族。省会太原市。

山西省地处黄河中游地区，一般海拔1000米左右，故通称山西高原；山区面积占全省面积70%左右，主要山脉有太行山、吕梁山、中条山及佛教名山五台山等。

山西省风景名胜、文物古迹众多。大同、平遥、新绛、代县、祁县均被列为国家历史文化名城。主要旅游景点有世界文化遗产平遥古城、大同云冈石窟，风景名胜区五台山、恒山、黄河壶口瀑布等，以及太原晋祠、平遥双林寺、应县木塔、大同华严寺、浑源悬空寺等文物古迹。

Shanxi Province, abbreviated as *Jin*, is situated in northern China, and adjacent to Hebei, Henan, Inner Mongolia and Shaanxi. It is so-called for its location on the west side of Taihang Mountains. Covering an area of over 150,000 square kilometers, Shanxi has a population of 32.97 million, which embracies the Hans, Huis, Manchurians, Mongolians, and other ethnic peoples. Taiyuan is the capital city.

Shanxi on eastern side of the middle reaches of the Yellow River has an average altitude of 1,000 meters, and mountains make up 70% of the total area of the province, so it is generally known as the Shanxi Plateau. The main mountains in the province are Taihang, Luliang, Zhongtiao and the famous Buddhist Mountain — Wutai Mountain.

Shanxi is a province with many historical sites and cultural relics, as well as scenic areas. Datong, Pingyao, Xinjiang, Daixian and Qixian are listed as the national historical and cultural cities. Main tourist spots are: world cultural heritages sites — Ancient City of Pingyao and the Yungang Grottoes; scenic spots of Wutai Mountain, Hengshan Mountain, and Hukou Waterfalls of the Yellow River; cultural and historical sites such as Jin Shrine in Taiyuan, Shuanglin Temple in Pingyao, Wooden Pagoda of Yingxian, Huayan Temple in Datong, Midair Temple in Hunyuan, Niangzi, Pingxing, and Yanmen passes of the Great Wall.

黄河壶口瀑布
Hukou Waterfalls
of the Yellow River

2

2-4 云冈石窟　位于大同市西16公里武周山南，是中国最大的石窟之一。石窟依山而凿，气魄宏大，外观庄严，雕工细腻。东西绵延约一公里，现存大小洞窟53个，小龛1100多个，造像5.1万多尊。云冈石窟始建于北魏兴安二年（公元453年），距今已有1500多年的历史。2001年，云冈石窟被联合国教科文组织列入《世界遗产名录》。

Yungang Grottoes　The Yungang Grottoes, one of the largest grottoes in China, lies on the Mount Wuzhou in Datong City. Consisting of a number of honeycomb-shaped grottoes, it was carved into the slope of the mountain, extending about one kilometer from east to west. With the construction of it beginning in 453, the grottoes have a history of more than 1,500 years. There are 53 caves, over 1,100 Buddhist niches, and 51,000 sculptures altogether. In 2001, UNESCO added it on the List of World Heritage.

5-7 平遥古城　位于山西省中部，是一座具有2700多年历史的文化名城。古城始建于周朝（公元前1066年—公元前221年），明洪武三年（公元1370年）进行扩建，是中国现存历史最早、规模最大的古代县城原型，被誉为"明、清建筑艺术的历史博物馆"。

The Ancient City of Pingyao　Situated in the middle of Shanxi Province, Pingyao has a history of over 2,700 years. It was firstly built during the Zhou Dynasty (1066BC-221BC), and was expanded in 1370, the third year of the reign period of Ming Emperor Hongwu. It is the earliest and largest ancient city in China, and reputed as "the History Museum of Architectural Art of the Ming and Qing Dynasties".

8 晋祠　位于太原市西南25公里处悬瓮山麓，相传为纪念晋国开国君主叔虞所建。晋祠殿宇错落，古木参天，风景优美。其中圣母殿内43尊侍女彩像为宋代所塑造，与周柏、难老泉并称"晋祠三绝"。

Jin Shrine　The Jin Shrine stands at the foot of Xuanweng Mountain, 25 kilometers southwest of Taiyuan. It was built in memory of Shu Yu, the founding ruler of the State of Jin. The Jin Shrine is famous for its scenic beauty. All buildings in the shrine were laid out ingeniously and surrounded by ancient trees. In the Hall of Holy Mother are 43 statues of young maids sculptured in the Song Dynasty. The statues, the pines planted during the Zhou Dynasty and the Nanlao Spring are know as the three rarities of the Jin Shrine.

9–11 五台山 位于五台县西北，是中国四大佛教名山之一。因该山由五座山峰组成，峰顶平坦如台，故名。最高峰北台海拔3058米，素称"华北屋脊"。五台山在东汉年间即有寺庙建筑，现存寺庙47处，所建年代及形制各不相同，是中国保存寺庙最多、最完整的佛教名山，也是中国佛教活动的重要场所之一。

Wutai Mountain Located in the northwest of Wutai County, the Mountain is one of the Four Most Famous Buddhist Mountains in China. It consists of five plat-like peaks, hence the name. The highest peak, North Plat, has an altitude of 3,058 meters, so it is nicknamed as the "Roof of North China". As early as during the Eastern Han Dynasty, there were temples built here. The 47 temples and the monasteries existing at present, built in different dynasties and in various styles, have turned the Wutai Mountain into a center of activities for Chinese Buddhist.

12

12 悬空寺　位于恒山天峰岭、翠屏峰之间峰壁之上，始建于北魏晚期。整个寺庙悬空而建，最高处离地面50米左右，犹如悬挂于悬崖绝壁之上，异常壮观▓寺内现存各式建筑40多间，并有各种铜铸、铁铸、泥塑、石刻造像78尊。

Midair Temple   First built during the Northern Wei Dynasty, the Midair Temple is located at the cliff between the peaks of Tianfengling and the Cuipingfeng of the Hengshan Mountains. The whole temple was built on the rock face of a sheer cliff, and the highest place in the temple is about 50 meters above ground, like suspending on the cliff face. The temple has more than 40 halls and rooms, housing 78 bronze, iron, colored clay and stone statues.

13 洪洞县大槐树公园
Park of the Big Chinese Scholar-Tree,
Hongdong County

13

14、15 华严寺　位于大同市西南，因属于佛教华严宗之寺庙，故名。该寺为辽金时期我国华严宗最重要的寺庙之一，分为上、下两处，布局严整，宏伟壮观。其中，下华严寺大殿内四周的两层楼阁式的藏经柜，结构极其精巧，为海内外孤品。

Huayan Temple　Located in southwest of Datong City, the temple is one of the most important temples of the Huayan Sect of Buddhism during the Liao and Jin dynasties, hence the name. The magnificent temple is divided into the upper and lower parts, both in great layout. The Cabinets of Storing Sutra in the Grand Hall of the Lower Huayan Temple, in two-storey-pavilion style, are ingeniously constructed and unique in the world.

16

16 黄河壶口瀑布　位于吉县西南25公里处黄河之中。黄河奔流至此，被两岸山峦夹峙收成一束，形成气势恢宏的瀑布奇观，一般落差在20米左右，惊涛怒吼，波浪翻腾，咆哮之声震耳欲聋。

Hukou Waterfalls of the Yellow River　The Hukou (Pot Spout) Waterfalls is situated at 25 kilometers west of Jixian County. When the Yellow River flows to the place, the water of the river is squeezed by mountains on both banks into a narrow gorge like the spout of a pot and rush rapidly, forming the grand waterfalls with a height of 20 meters. The mountains echo with the deafening sound of the roaring water, which could be heard several kilometers away.

17 娘子关
　Niangzi Pass of the Great Wall

18 平型关
　Pingxing Pass of the Great Wall

19 北岳恒山　位于浑源县南10公里，主峰海拔2017米，被誉为"绝塞名山"。恒山分为东西两峰，东为天峰岭，西为翠屏峰，双峰对峙，山势险峻，自古即为兵家必争之地，其地貌有"常山如行"的特点。恒山风景区风光秀丽，是国务院公布的第一批国家重点风景名胜区之一。主要景点有悬空寺、三清殿、九天宫等。

Hengshan Mountain　Hengshan Mountain, the northern Sacred Mountain, rises 10 kilometers south of Hunyuan County, and is famed as "the famous mountain of the strategic importance". The mountain consists of two peaks: the Tianfengling on the east and the Cuipingfeng on the west. The two peaks stand facing each other, and form a precipitous natural barrier, where was a place contested by all strategists. The terrain of the mountain is characterized by "parallel lines of mountains". The Hengshan Mountain Scenic Area was inscribed on the first list of major scenic areas and historical sites in the country proclaimed by the State Council. Major tourist attractions include the Midair Temple, Hall of Pure Trinity, Nine-Heaven Palace, Flying-Stone Grottoes, and so on.

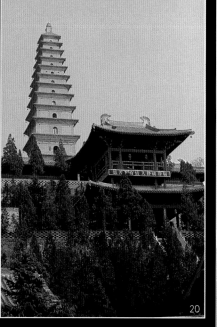

20 普救寺莺莺塔
Yingying Pagoda in the Temple of
Universal Rescue

21 应县木塔　位于应县佛宫寺内。木塔始建于辽代清宁二年（公元1056年），平面八角形，高67.13米，塔底直径30.27米，是世界现存最古老、最高大的木结构塔式建筑。木塔外观5层，夹有暗层4层，塔内有彩塑、壁画等文物。

Wooden Pagoda of Ying County　The Wooden Pagoda, standing in the Temple of Buddhist Palace in Ying County, was originally built in 1056 (the ond year of Qingning reign of the Liao Dynasty). The octagonal pagoda is 67.13 meters high and 30.27 meters in diameter at the foundation, which makes it the oldest and tallest of its kind. From the outside, the pagoda appears to be a five-storied building with six layers of eaves, but four stores are hidden. It houses many cultural relics such as color-sculptures and frescoes.

22 永乐宫　位于芮城县北3公里，是中国现存最早的道教宫观之一。现存建筑除宫门为清代建筑，其余均为元代所修。宫内保存有元代精美壁画，总面积达960平方米，是中国绘画史上的杰作。

Yongle Palace　Yongle Palace, or the Palace of Eternal Joy, situated 3 kilometers to the north of Ruicheng County, is one of the earliest Taoist complexes in China. All buildings in the palace were constructed during the Yuan Dynasty except the gate which was built during the Qing Dynasty. Also preserved in the palace are beautiful mural paintings of the Yuan Dynasty. The mural paintings cover a total of 960 square meters, and are the finest works in the history of Chinese painting.

内蒙古自治区
INNER MONGOLIA AUTONOMOUS REGION

内蒙古自治区简称内蒙古，位于中国北部、西北部边疆，与俄罗斯和蒙古两国交界。全区面积110多万平方公里，人口2367万，有蒙古、汉、达斡尔、鄂温克、鄂伦春、回、满、朝鲜等民族，其中，蒙古族人口占全区的九分之一。内蒙古1947年成立自治区，是中国最早建立的民族自治区。首府呼和浩特市。

内蒙古草原风光十分迷人，民族风情独具特色。东部的大兴安岭原始森林被称为"绿色宝库"，是野生动植物的王国。主要旅游景区有成吉思汗陵、昭君墓、五当召等。每年7月和8月间举行那达慕草原旅游节，有赛马、射箭、摔跤、马术、民族歌舞等项目，是蒙古族最隆重的传统节日盛会，可使游人在美丽如画的草原上领略马背民族的风情。

Abbreviated as *Neimenggu* (Inner Mongolia), the region extends across north and northwest frontier of China, bordering on Russia and the Republic of Mongolia. The over 1.1-million-square-kilometer region is home to ethnic peoples including Mongolians which making up one-ninth of the total, Hans, Daurs, Ewenkis, Oroqens, Huis, Manchurians, Koreans, and others, with a total population of 23.67 million. Found-ed in 1947, it is the first ethic autonomous region in China. The capital is Hohhot City.

The region abounds in tourist attractions of beautiful scenery of grassland and unique folklore. Daxing'anling in the eastern of the region, reputed as "the Green Treasure House", is a kingdom of wild animals. The region has many attractions to offer, including Mausoleum of Genghis Khan, Tomb of Princess Zhaojun, and Wudangzhao. Horse-racing, archery, wrestling, horsemanship, folk singing and dancing, are main items for Nadam Festival, the foremost traditional festival of Mongol nomads, taking place every year, which would help visitors to know about culture of the people on horseback.

1 草原风光
The grassland landscape

2 成吉思汗陵　坐落在伊金霍洛旗境内，距包头 185 公里处。主体建筑是仿照元代城楼式的门亭和三个互相连通的蒙古包式大殿，分为 20 多米高的中央纪念堂、东西配殿、东西走廊和寝宫六部分。堂后寝宫内供奉着装饰华丽的成吉思汗夫妇灵柩，每年都在此举行公祭活动。

Mausoleum of Genghis Khan The mausoleum is found in Ejan Horo Banner, 185 kilometers south of Baotou. The main buildings include a gate arch imitating the style of a Yuan period's city tower and three inter-linking yurt-style great halls, involving a 20-meter-high memorial hall in center, and the east and west side halls together with east and west corridors in addition to a bedroom palace. The remains of Genghis Khan, a pre-eminent 12th-century Mongolian monarch(1162-1227), and his wife are enshrined in the bedroom palace behind the memorial hall. The entire complex is splendidly ornamented. Sacrifice ceremonies held annually here, to commemorate the great hero and leader of the Mongolian people.

3 黄河上中游交界处
Boundary between the upper and middle reaches of the Yellow River

4 五塔寺
Five-Pagoda Lamasery
5 额济纳旗风光
Scenery of Ejina Banner
6 呼和浩特市景
A view of Hohhot
7 敖包
Obo (a three-tiered conical stone mound)

8、9 昭君墓　位于呼和浩特市南 9 公里处，占地 1.3 万平方米，墓高 33 米。因深秋季节北方草木皆枯，而墓上草绿如茵，又名"青冢"。

　　王昭君，名嫱，汉元帝时自愿嫁给匈奴呼韩邪单于，充当和亲使者，为民族团结做出了贡献。此后四十余年里，两国和平相处，没有战事发生。

Tomb of Princess Zhaojun　　Located 9 kilometers to the south of Hohhot proper, the cemetery covers an area of 1.3 hectare. The tomb is 33 meters high. It was said that each year when it turned cold and grasses became yellow, only this tomb remained green, so it was also called "Qingzhong" (Green Tomb).

　　Wang Zhaojun, also named Wang Qiang, married Huhanye Chanyu, the emperor of Xiongnu, of her own free will during the reign period of Emperor Yuan of the Han Dynasty. She made great contributions to the relationship between Han and Xiongnu, and in the following more than 40 years, no wars broke out and people of both countries lived a peaceful life.

10

10 五当召 位于包头市东北约70公里处，原名巴达嘎尔庙，是内蒙古地区保存最完整的藏式佛教庙宇之一，也是该地区最大的黄教寺院。该寺初建于清康熙年间，依山势布局，现存殿宇僧舍2500余间，主要由六殿三府一陵组成。

Wudangzhao Wudangzhao, or the Bad Ger Lamasery, lying 70 kilometers southwest of Baotou, is one of the best-preserved Tibetan-style lamaseries and largest Tibetan Buddhist monastery of the Yellow Sect (Gelugpa) in the entire autonomous region. Situating on a hill slope and built during the Kangxi's reign (1662-1722) of the Qing Dynasty, it is a vast complex consisting of six main halls, three Living Buddha mansions and a mausoleum, and has a total of 2,500 rooms.

11 达赉湖
　 Dalai Lake

11

12

12-15 草原旅游区 内蒙古自治区草原面积88万平方公里，占中国草原面积的21.7%，居全国五大草原之首。从东到西分布着草甸草原、典型草原、荒漠草原、草原化荒漠和荒漠，以及零星分布于各地的山地草甸、低湿地草甸和沼泽草场等草地类型。内蒙古的主要草原旅游区有呼伦贝尔、锡林郭勒、希拉穆仁、辉腾锡勒、格根塔拉等。每年5月至9月间，绿草如茵，鲜花遍地，牛羊成群，河湖遍布，蒙古族居住的蒙古包像珍珠般点缀其间，构成了一幅极其壮美的图画。

Grassland Tourist Zones   In the Inner Mongolia Autonomous Region, the area of grassland is 880,000 square kilometers, or accounting for 21.7 per cent of the nation's total, the leading of China's five largest grasslands. From east to west, are scattered grassy marshland, typical grassland, wilderness grassland, grassy willderness, and desert as well as hilly grassy marshlands, low wet and grassy marshland, and marshy grassland,distributed randomly anywhere. Major grassland tourist zones include the Hulunbuir, Xilin Gol, Xila Muren, Huiteng Xile and Gegen Tala. From May to September, the lands are covered with green grass and flowers, with big berds of cattle and sheep grazing in the meadows, ribbon-like rivers, pearl-like lakes and yurts resided by the mongolians. They all constitute beautiful and majestic pictures.

13

14

15

辽宁省
LIAONING PROVINCE

辽宁省简称辽，位于中国东北地区南部，东南隔鸭绿江与朝鲜相邻，南临黄、渤二海，与山东半岛隔海相望，地形险要，是守卫京津的门户。全省面积15万多平方公里，人口4238万，有汉、蒙古、朝鲜、锡伯等民族。省会沈阳市。

辽宁省东北部和东部，系由长白山余脉和千山山脉构成，中部为著名的辽河平原，南端辽东半岛是水果生产基地，辽西锦州一带沿海有百余公里长的"走廊"，是关内外交通孔道。

辽宁省历史文化悠久，名胜古迹众多，自然风光优美，旅游资源十分丰富。全省现有国家级文物保护单位191处，历史遗址和纪念地70余处。主要风景名胜区有千山、鸭绿江游览区、大连海滨、棒槌岛、医巫闾山、本溪水洞、兴城海滨等；名胜古迹有：沈阳故宫、昭陵、福陵，鞍山玉佛苑等。

Abbreviated as "*Liao*", the province is the southern part of area of northeast China, separated from Korea by the Yalu River in its southeast. It faces the Shandong Peninsula across the Yellow Sea and Bohai Sea in the south, making it a strategic gateway to Beijing and Tianjin. Covering a total of 150,000 square kilometers, the province has a population of 42.38 million of Hans, Mongolians, Koreans, Xibos and other ethnic peoples. The provincial capital is Shenyang.

Liaoning is covered by wooded mountains of Changbai and Qianshan in the northeast and east, the vast Liaohe plain is in its heart. The Liaodong Peninsula in the south is famous production base of fruits, and the West Liaoning Corridor — a narrow strip of plain along a hundreds-of-kilometer-long coast of the Bohai Sea.

Liaoning is a province with long history, multitudinous historical relics and beautiful scenery — all these forming it rich resources of tourism. There are 191 cultural sites under national or provincial protection in the province, and 70-odd historical monuments and relics. Major scenic resorts include Qianshan Mountain, Yalu River and Dalian Beach scenic areas, Wooden-Club Isle, Yiwulu Mountain, Pen-Rest Mountain in Jinzhou, Water Cave in Benxi, and Beach of Xingcheng. Main places of historical interest are Shenyang Imperial Palace, Zhaoling Mausoleum, Fuling Mausoleum, Jade Buddha Park, Hushan Section of the Great Wall, and so on.

1 大连港夜景
Dalian at night

2-4 沈阳故宫　位于沈阳旧城中心，建于1625年至1636年，是清太祖努尔哈赤及清太宗皇太极营建的皇宫，顺治帝也在此登基。故宫占地约6万平方米，有房屋300多间，主要建筑有崇政殿、大政殿、凤凰楼和清宁宫等。

Shenyang Imperial Palace　Located in the center of old town of Shenyang, the palace was first constructed by orders of Nurhachi, the former founder of the Manchurian Empire and the Qing Dynasty, in 1625 and completed in 1636 under the reign of Abahai, his eighth son. It was here that Qing Emperor Shunzhi was crowned before setting off to cross the Great Wall in 1644. Covering an area of 60,000 square meters and

having more than 300 halls and rooms, it is considered a miniature of the Forbidden City in Beijing. But it by comparison is smaller in scale and the Manchurian influence behind its construction shows a vast departure in style from its predecessor. Main buildings are Chongzhengdian (the Hall of Devoted Affairs), Dazhengdian (the Hall of Great Affairs), Fenghuanglou (the Phoenix Tower) and Qingninggong (the Palace of Celestial Peace).

5、6 北陵　即昭陵，是清太宗皇太极和其皇后的陵墓，因地处沈阳北郊故名 ■■ 福陵、永陵并称"关外三陵"。陵墓占地18万平方米，竣工于清顺治八年（公元1651年），集满、汉、蒙古民族建筑艺术于一体。现已扩建为北陵公园。

Northern Mausoleum　Also known as Zhaoling, it got the present name from its location in northern suburbs of Shenyang city, and was called "the Three Mausoleums of the Qing Dynasty out of Shanhai Pass", along with Fuling and Yongling tombs. Covering a total of 180,000 square meters, it was the tomb of Qing Emperor Abahai and his wife. Completed in 1651, or the eighth year of Emperor Shunzhi's reign, it is an integration of Manchu, Han and Mongolia architectural arts.

7 鞍山大玉佛
World's largest Jade Buddha in Anshan
8 大连文化广场
Culture Square, Dalian
9 大连星海广场
Star Sea Square, Dalian
10 大连有轨电车
Tramcar in Dalian
11 沈阳大帅府内景
Interior of the Marshal Mansion
(former residence of Zhang Zuolin and
Zhang Xueliang), Shenyang
12 鸭绿江
The Yalu River

大连市 位于辽东半岛南端，是中国北方旅游和疗养胜地。全市面积1.2万多平方公里，人口500多万。大连三面环海，气候宜人，海滨自然风光绝佳，城市干净美丽，是著名的避暑和旅游城市，也是国家风景名胜区。主要风景区有棒槌岛、老虎滩公园、傅家庄公园、星海公园、金石滩风景区和旅顺口风景区等。

Dalian   The beautiful seaside city of Dalian on the southern tip of Liaodong Peninsula is a nice sightseeing recuperating and holidaymaking destination. It has an area of 1.2 hectares and a population of 5 million. Skirted on three sides by the sea, Dalian owns fabulous seaside landscape, pleasant weather and neat and beautiful urban environment, being a celebrated summering place and tourist city, as well as a national scenic resort. Main scenic spots include Bangchui (Wooden-Club) Isle, Laohutan (Tiger's Beach) Park, Fujiazhuang Park, Xinghai (Star Sea) Park, Jinshitan (Golden Rock) Beach and lushunkou Scenic Resort and so on.

14 千山　位于鞍山市东南，距市中心约20公里处，又名千朵莲花山；林木葱茏，植被丰富，为国家级风景名胜区。近年，在景区内又发现一尊由整座山峰形成的天然弥勒佛坐像，高70余米，在大佛脚下还发掘出明、清两代的供器，而成为东北地区的佛教圣地。

Qianshan Mountain　Also called "A-Thousand-Lotus-Flower Mountain", it is located southeast of Anshan, 20 kilometers from city proper. The mountain is densely wooded, and abounds in flora and fauna, and is a national scenic resort. Among its scenic spots is a new discovery — a nature statue of the Buddha forming by a peak, which stands 70 meters high. The place has since become a holy land of Buddhism in northeast China. And many sacrificial utensils of the Ming and Qing dynasties were discovered at the foot of the peak.

13 兴城海滨
   Xingcheng Beach
15 锦州笔架山〝天桥〞
   "Heavenly Bridge" on the Pen-Rest
   Mountain, Jinzhou
16 虎山长城
   Hushan Section of the Great Wall

中国风景名胜

吉林省
JILIN PROVINCE

吉林省简称吉，位于中国东北地区的中部、松花湖畔，东南与俄罗斯、朝鲜相邻。"吉林"，满语为"沿江"的意思。全省面积18万多平方公里，人口2728万，主要有汉、朝鲜、满、蒙古、锡伯等民族。省会长春市。

吉林省地势东南高西北低，中西部为平原。东南部长白山区一般海拔1000米以上。著名的松花江全长900多公里，发源于白头山天池。鸭绿江和图们江发源于长白山脉，是中朝两国的界河。

吉林省的重要城市有省会、"汽车城"长春，历史文化名城吉林、集安，延边朝鲜族自治州首府延吉等。名胜有长白山、天池、松花湖、净月潭风景区、长春电影城、伪皇宫等。

Jilin, a province abbreviated as "Ji", is located in the center of northeast China by Songhua Lake, adjacent to countries as Russia and Korea in the southeast. Its name means "By the River" in the Manchu language. The province is 180,000 square kilometers in area with a population of 27.28 million including Han, Korea, Manchu, Mongol, Xibo and other ethic peoples. Changchun is the provincial capital.

Topographically, Jilin is high in the southeast and low in the northwest, with a plain in its western part. The Changbai Mountain, rising in the southeastern part of the province, is 1,000 meters above sea level in average altitude. The famous 900-kilometer-long Songhua River rises from the Tianchi Lake on the White-Headed Mountain. Yalu and Tumen rivers, both rising from the Changbai Mountain, are the boundary rivers between China and Korea.

Major cities of Jilin include "the Auto City"— Changchun, the famous historical and cultural cities of Jilin and Ji'an, and Yanji, capital of Yanbian Korean Autonomous Prefecture. Main tourist spots in the province are Changbai Mountain, Tianchi Lake, Songhua Lake, Jingyue Pool, Puppet State's Imperial Palace, Motion Picture City, and so on.

1 长白山
Changbai Mountain

2 长白山自然保护区 长白山位于吉林省东南部、中朝两国交界处，是以自然风光和动植物资源为特色的中国名山之一，主峰海拔2691米。自然保护区面积2000多平方公里，是一座大型的天然植物园和动物园，有山峰、林海、天池、瀑布、温泉等风景名胜，被联合国教科文组织纳入"国际人与生物圈保护计划"。

Changbai Mountain Nature Reserve Lying in southeastern Jilin Province, the junction of China and Korea, Changbai Mountain is famous for its beautiful scenery and rich resources of animals and plants. The main peak, Baitou (White-Headed) Peak, is 2,691 meters above sea level. Covering a total of 2,000 square kilometers, Changbai Mountain Nature Reserve, a mammoth natural zoo and botanical garden, is part of the UNESCO's Man and Biosphere Program. Peaks, sea of forests, Tianchi Lake, waterfalls and hot springs are local natural wonders.

3 净月潭公园 位于长春市东南15公里处，面积约150平方公里，为亚洲最大的人造森林之一和国家森林公园，是旅游观光、度假休闲、康复疗养的好去处。公园内有山峰86座，净月潭面积4.3平方公里，被誉为台湾日月潭的"姐妹湖"。

Jingyue (Clear Moon) Pool Park 15 kilometers southeast from Changchun downtown and 150 square kilometers in area, it is one of the largest artificial forests in Asia and a national forest park where the ecological system is well protected. The place, with a total of 86 peaks, has become a scenic resort where holidaymakers go for sightseeing, recuperating, recreation, and other purposes. The 4.3-square-kilometer Jingyue Pool is regard as a "sister" to Taiwan's Riyue (Sun and Moon) Pool.

4 长春伪皇宫
Puppet State's Imperial Palace, Changchun

5、6 吉林雾凇　与桂林山水、云南石林和长江三峡并称中国四大自然奇特景观。雾凇，俗称"树挂"，即使隆冬时节，松花江水仍缓缓流淌，蒸腾的雾气遇寒冷的空气凝结于树枝上，形成了这一神奇景观。

Rimed Trees in Jilin　The rimed trees of Jilin are extolled as one of four major natural wonders of China along with the landscape of Guilin, the Stone Forest of Yunnan, and the Three Gorges of the Yangtze River. In winter, the Songhua River keeps flowing through Jilin despite the subfreezing temperature, and the vapour rising from the surface of the river freezes when it meets the branches of pines and willows ashore. Thus encrusted with layers upon layers of ice, the tree branches and twigs look transparent and form a spectacular crystal world.

7 长春文化广场
　Culture Square, Changchun
8 松花江晚霞
　Songhua River at sunset

9 长白山天池　海拔 2194 米，是中国最高的火山湖，也是中朝两国的界湖。湖面面积近 10 平方公里，平均水深 204 米，群峰环抱，景色优美。

Tianchi Lake of Changbai Mountain　Tianchi Lake, or the Heavenly Lake, with an elevation of 2,194 meters, is the highest volcanic lake in China. Almost 10 square kilometers in area and 204 meters in average depth, it marks the boundary of China and Korea. Skirted on all sides by mountains, the lake is known for its sublime natural beauty.

黑龙江省
HEILONGJIANG PROVINCE

黑 龙江省位于中国东北的最北部，简称黑█，全省面积46万多平方公里，人口3689万，有汉、满、蒙古、回、朝鲜、鄂伦春、赫哲等民族。省会哈尔滨市。

黑龙江省境内江山壮美，一派北国风光。兴安山区林海莽莽，是著名的森林旅游区和天然狩猎场。该省为中国火山遗址地较多的省区之一，火山活动创造了其独特的旅游资源，五大连池素有"火山地质博物馆"之称。扎龙自然保护区沼泽地是丹顶鹤群集地，被誉为"仙鹤故乡"。此外，还有松花江游览区、镜泊湖吊水楼瀑布、唐渤海国上京遗址等名胜。黑龙江冬季漫长而寒冷，夏季短促而日照充足。寒冷的气候赋予了其得天独厚的冰雪资源。严冬时节是冰雪活动的黄金季节，█有滑冰橇、冬泳、溜冰、打冰猴等众多项目；巧夺天工的冰雕更堪称是北国一大奇观。玉泉山、亚布力等滑雪场也是游客休闲度假的好去处。

Heilongjiang Province, abbreviated as *Hei*, is located at the northernmost tip of China. This province of 460,000 square kilometers is populated by 36.89 million of Hans, Manchurians, Mongolians, Huis, Koreans, Oroqens, Hezhens, and other peoples. Harbin is the provincial capital.

The beautiful mountains and rivers in Heilongjiang present magnificent northern scenery. In dense forests on the Xing'anling Mountains are forests resorts and natural hunting grounds. The province is abundant in volcanic ruins. The volcanic eruptions created Heilongjiang unique and spectacular tourist resources. Lake Wudalianchi is known as "the Museum of Volcanic Geology". The marsh of Zhalong Nature Reserve, where red-rested cranes gather, is reputed as "the home to cranes". Among Heilongjiang's other tourist resources are Songhua River, Diaoshuilou Waterfalls of Jingpo Lake, and Ruins of Ancient State Bohai of the Tang Dynasty. The province has long and cold winters and short summers with plenty sunshine. And the frigid climate bestows Heilongjiang rich resources of ice and snow. Winters are golden seasons for ice and snow programs including skiing, winter swimming, skating, ice hockey, and so on. Also the exquisite ice and snow sculptures are known as a spectacular of the North. Up to present, the Yabuli and Yuquan Mountain skiing grounds are ideal places for tourists to spend a holiday.

1 哈尔滨冰灯
Ice lights in Harbin

6 圣·索菲亚教堂 始建于1907年，通高53.35米，面积720余平方米，是远东地区最大的东正教堂。教堂为砖木结构，风格受拜占庭式建筑影响，富丽堂皇，典雅超俗。

St. Sophia Church First built in 1907, the church, 53.35 meters in height and 720 square meters in area, is the largest Eastern Orthodox Church in the Far East. The splendid and elegant structure of bricks and wood shows a strong influence of the Byzantine style of architecture.

2 哈尔滨冬景
  Winter scenery of Harbin
3 哈尔滨冰雕
  Ice sculpture in Harbin
4、5 亚布力滑雪场
  Yabuli Skiing Ground

7 镜泊湖 位于宁安市境内，距牡丹江市110公里。湖面海拔350米，面积95平方公里，是中国最大的高山湖之一。群山环抱，景色秀丽。位于湖北端的吊水楼瀑布，最大落差25米，飞瀑直泻，尤为壮观。

Jingpo Lake Lying in Ning'an and 110 kilometers from Mudanjiang City, the 95-square-kilometer Jingpo Lake is one of the largest alpine lakes in China, at an altitude of 350 meters above sea level. Embraced by rolling mountains, the lake is famous for beautiful scenery. The Diaoshuilou Watefalls, located in northern part of the lake, rushes down with a height of 25 meters, forming a spectacular scene.

上海市
SHANGHAI MUNICIPALITY

上海市位于中国东部海岸中段、长江入海口，总面积5800平方公里，是中国四大直辖市之一，人口1674万。上海市简称沪，春秋战国时期，曾为楚国春申君黄歇的封地，故又别称"申城"。

上海市地处长江三角洲平原东端，扼守长江出口，是中国重要的门户，17世纪即成为一个繁盛的港口。现为太平洋地区重要的国际港口城市，也是中国最大的商业、金融中心，内、外贸易额均居全国各大贸易中心首位。

上海市历史悠久，是中国历史文化名城之一，也是著名的国际化大都市，旅游资源丰富多彩。主要名胜有豫园、玉佛寺、龙华寺、嘉定孔庙、吴淞口炮台、中共一大会址等；现代景观有南浦大桥、东方明珠广播电视塔、杨浦大桥、新外滩、南京路、陆家嘴、浦东新区、上海大剧院、上海博物馆等。

One of China's four municipalities directly under the Central Government, Shanghai is located in the middle of the coast of the Chinese mainland and on the southern shore of the Yangtze River estuary. The city, 5,800 square kilometers in area, has a population of 16.74 million. It is abbreviated as "*Hu*", also nicknamed "Shencheng" because the land was the manor of Huang Xie, Duke Chunshen of the Chu State during the Spring and Autumn and Warring States periods.

Situated in the eastern part of the Yangtze River Delta, Shanghai holds the mouth of the Yangtze River, making it an important gateway to China. The city became a busy port as early as in the 17th century. Today, it is one of the most important international port cities in the Pacific Region, as well as a major commercial and financial center of China, and ranks first among the country's centers of domestic and foreign trade.

One of famous historical and cultural cities in China and noted internationalized metropolis, Shanghai has a long history and is rich in tourist resources. Among the major attractions and historical sites in the city are Yuyuan Garden, Yufo (Jade Buddha)Temple, Longhua Temple, Confucius Temple in Jiading District, Wusongkou Fort and Site of the First National Congress of the Chinese Communist Party. New developed tourist attractions include Yangpu and Nanpu bridges, the Oriental Pearl TV Tower, New Bund, Nanjing Road, Lujiazui, New Pudong District, Shanghai Grand Theatre, Shanghai Museum, and so on.

1 东方明珠广播电视塔
Broadcasting and Television
Tower of Oriental Pearl

2 东方明珠广播电视塔　坐落在陆家嘴，总高度468米，是上海的标志性建筑。塔主体由3个斜筒体、3个直筒体和11个球体组成，设计独具匠心，集旅游、购物、娱乐、餐饮和广播电视功能于一体。

Broadcasting and Television Tower of Oriental Pearl　Shortened as the Oriental Pearl TV Tower, it is situated in the tip of Lujiazui. 468 meters in height, the tower is Shanghai's landmark and a big magnet for tourists. The high tower is supported by 3 columns and 3 oblique braces, and 11 beautiful spheres of various sizes are set magically, like eleven shining pearls embedded on the body of the tower. It is a multi-functional establishment, and is equipped with tourist service facilities, including eateries, shops, recreational centers and a hotel.

3 陆家嘴
Lujiazui
4 外滩夜景
The Bund at Night

5 上海大剧院　造型独特美观，是上海的标志性建筑之一。大剧院建筑面积6.2万多平方米，总高度40米，共有10层。每当夜晚，它就像一座水晶宫殿，晶莹透亮，具有强烈的时代感。

Shanghai Grand Theatre　The theatre has become a representative building in Shanghai for its unique style and beautiful outlook. With a total construction area of more than 62,000 square meters and a total height of 40 meters, it has 10 storeys, 2 for underground, 2 for lofts and 6 on the ground. When night falls, the crystal-like theater glitters in infinite brilliance, giving people an impression of metropolitan art.

6 南浦大桥
Nanpu Bridge
7 南京路夜景
A night scene of Nanjing Road
8 石库门
Shikumen Residences
9 中国共产党第一次全国代表大会会址
Site of the First National Congress of the
Chinese Communist Party

10

12

10、11 豫园 始建于明嘉靖三十八年（公元1559年），设计精巧，风景优美，建筑精致，是上海著名的江南古典园林。全园有景点40余处，被蜿蜒曲折的五龙墙分割成6个景区。

Yuyuan Garden　Built in 1559, or the 38th year of the Ming Emperor Jiajing's reign,

Yuyuan is the most celebrated classical Chinese garden in Shanghai. It is character-ized by an exquisite layout, beautiful scenery and artistic architecture. There are more than 40 scenic spots scattered throughout this garden. The wandering Five-Dragon-Wall subdivides the garden into six regions.

12 玉佛寺玉佛
Jade Buddha Statue in the Yufo Temple

江苏省
JIANGSU PROVINCE

江苏省简称苏，位于中国东南沿海，跨华北平原和长江下游平原。全省面积10万多平方公里，人口7400多万，有汉、回、满等民族。省会南京市。

江苏省河湖众多，苏南太湖、苏北洪泽湖周围水网密布，有"水乡泽国"之称。又因气候温和，土地肥沃，素有"鱼米之乡"的美誉。

江苏省旅游资源极为丰富，是山水园林、名胜古迹高度集中的地区，也是中国历史文化名城最多的省份，主要有南京、镇江、常熟、苏州、扬州、徐州、淮安等。著名胜迹和风景区有世界文化遗产苏州古典园林和南京明孝陵，全国重点风景名胜区太湖、钟山、云台山、瘦西湖等，江南水乡周庄、同里、用直，以及中山陵、镇江三山、灵山大佛和寒山寺等。

Abbreviated as "*Su*", Jiangsu Province lies in China's southeastern coastal region spanning the Huabei (North China) Plain and the Plain of the Lower Reaches of the Yangtze River. It covers an area of over 100,000 square kilometers, with a population of 74 million, comprising mainly of Hans, Huis, and Manchurians ethnic peoples. The provincial capital is Nanjing.

The province is crisscrossed by rivers and studded with lakes. Southern Jiangsu is drained by a network of rivers and streams around Taihu Lake, and northern Jiangsu, by those around Hongze Lake, so the province is known as a "region of rivers and lakes". And its mild climate and fertile soil win it a nickname: "the land of fish and rice".

Abounding in places of historical interest and scenic beauty, Jiangsu has rich resources of tourism. The province has seven national famous historical and cultural cities — Nanjing, Zhenjiang, Changsu, Suzhou, Yangzhou, Xuzhou and Huaian. Major tourist spots and scenic resorts are world heritage sites — classical gardens of Suzhou and Ming Xiaoling Mausoleum, the national scenic resorts of Taihu Lake, Bell Mountain, Yuntai Mountain, Lean West Lake, water counties of Zhouzhuang, Tongli and Luzhi, and others including Mausoleum of Dr Sun Yat-sen, three hills in Zhenjiang, Giant Buddha of Lingshan, and Cool-Hill Temple.

1 苏州狮子林
Shizilin (Lion-Forest Garden),
Suzhou

2 苏州网师园
  Wangshiyuan (Garden of the Master-of-the-Nets), Suzhou

3 苏州古典园林　苏州位于江苏省东南部，市内河道交错，拱桥众多，被誉为"东方威尼斯"。苏州园林集中了江南园林的精华，具有宋、元、明、清历代不同风格的园林。园林设计巧妙，在有限的空间内将园林建造得小巧秀丽，朴素精巧。其中，沧浪亭、狮子林、拙政园、留园被称作"苏州四大名园"。1997年，苏州古典园林被联合国教科文组织列入《世界遗产名录》。

Classical Gardens of Suzhou　Suzhou is located in the southeast of Jiangsu Province, and is called "Venice of the East" for its criss-cross rivers and many arched-bridges. The classical gardens in Suzhou represent the quintessence of the gardens built in southern area of the Yangtze River, and demonstrate the varied styles of Song, Yuan, Ming and Qing dynasties. The gardens are not large but fascinating in their delicate design. The Canglangting, Shizilin, Zhuozhengyuan, and Liuyuan are four most famous gardens in Suzhou. In 1997, UNESCO inscribed the Classical Gardens of Suzhou on the List of World Heritage.

4 苏州拙政园
Zhuozhengyuan
(Humble Administrator's Garden), Suzhou
5 苏州网师园
Wangshiyuan
(Garden of the Master-of-the-Nets), Suzhou
6 苏州沧浪亭
Canglangting
(Surging Wave Pavilion), Suzhou
7 苏州拙政园
Zhuozhengyuan
(Humble Administrator's Garden), Suzhou
8、9 同里退思园
Tuisiyuan
(Garden of Retreat and Reflection), Tongli

10、11 明孝陵　位于南京市紫金山南麓，是明代开国皇帝朱元璋及其皇后的陵墓，建于1383年。主要建筑有四方城、孝陵殿、宝城等。陵前半部有一条1800米长的神路，两旁有石兽、望柱、翁仲等雕像。2003年，明孝陵被联合国教科文组织列入《世界遗产名录》。

Ming Xiaoling Mausoleum　Lying on the south slope of Mount Zijin (Purple Gold), it is the tomb of Zhu Yuanzhang, founder of the Ming Dynasty, and his wife. Built in 1383, main buildings in the mausoleum include the Square City, Hall of Xiaoling, Precious City, and so on. On both sides of the 1800-meter-long winding sacred way are stone animal, minister and general statues. In 2003, UNESCO added it on the World Heritage List.

12　南京莫愁女塑像
　　Statue of the Girl of Mochou
　　(Don't Worry or Carefree)
13　南京中华门
　　Zhonghua (Chinese) Gate, Nanjing
14　南京狮子山阅江楼
　　Tower of Viewing the River on the
　　Lion Mountain, Nanjing
15　南京中山陵
　　Mausoleum of Dr Sun Yat-sen, Nanjing

中国风景名胜

15

16 秦淮河 位于南京市西南，全长100多公里，为长江支流。内河曾为南京最繁华的地带，歌舞彻夜，彩船如织，热闹非凡，许多爱情故事都发生在这里。经过整修建设，秦淮河风光带现为南京最具特色的商业、旅游和民俗文化区。

Qinhuai River Southwest of the city of Nanjing and extending more than 100 kilometers, Qinhuai river is a branch of the Yangtze River. The inner section of the river used to be the most flourishing place of Nanjing. Painted boats shuttled to and flo and music sounded all night. Many love affairs and romances spread from here. Having been archaized and revived, nowadays, the region becomes the most characterized area of commerce, tourism and folklore and culture.

16

17

17　苏州虎丘
Tiger-Hill Park, Suzhou
18　苏州雪景
A snow scene of Suzhou
19　苏州枫桥
Maple Bridge, Suzhou
20　苏州寒山寺
Cold-Hill Temple, Suzhou
21　苏州一景
A view of Suzhou

22 周庄沈厅内景
　　Interior of the Mansion of Shen's Family

23—25 周庄　水乡古镇周庄位于昆山市西南，面积36平方公里。古镇已有900余年的历史，镇内保存着完好的宋代"水陆平行，河街相邻"的井字形格局，有"水中桃源"之美誉。全镇有近百座古宅大院，著名的有沈厅、张厅等。镇内河道上横跨着保存完好的元、明、清历代石桥14座。

Ancient Water Town of Zhouzhuang   Zhouzhuang is located to the southwest of Kunshan City, with an area of 36 square kilometers. It has a history of more than 900 years, and has preserved architectural style and layout of the Song Dynasty — "land and water routes running parallel, and streets and canals neighboring each other". It is reputed as "the Heaven of Peace on Water". Spanning on the rivers are 14 stone bridges dating back to the Yuan, Ming and Qing dynasties. There are nearly a hundred of ancient residences and compounds, and the most famous ones are the mansions of Shen's Family and Zhang's Family.

26

26-28 古镇同里　距苏州18公里，是目前江苏省保存最完整的水乡古镇之一。全镇总面积62平方公里，四面环水，是一座幽静的江南古镇，历来有"水镇桥乡"之称。镇区被15条小河分隔成7个圩头，49座古桥将小岛连成一个整体，街河并行，桥路相接，建筑傍水而立，户户临水通舟，街巷、民居、河桥融汇一体。

An Ancient Town of Tongli　Located on the lakeside of Taihu and the shore of the Great Canal, 18 kilometers to Suzhou, Tongli, a picturesque and elegant town covering an area of 62 square kilometers, has become world-known for its wonderful scenery and classic buildings. It is surrounded by water on four sides. The proper of this town is divided into seven blocks by 15 rivers, and 49 ancient bridges in different designs and sizes combine them into a complete whole. With their dwellings built beside the stream, the locals all enjoys the convenience to travel by boat. Tongli is rich in both culture relics and

28

traditional architectures, there are many classic buildings constructed during the Ming and Qing dynasties. The Tuisi Garden (the Garden of Retreat and Reflection) is the most famous one.

27

29 镇江宋街
   Song Dynasty Street, Zhenjiang
30 镇江金山寺
   Golden Mountain Temple, Zhenjiang
31 太湖风光
   Scenery of Taihu Lake

33

34

32 扬州五亭桥
Five-Pavilion Bridge, Yangzhou
33 扬州野春园
Wild-Spring Garden, Yangzhou
34 扬州大明寺
Daming Temple, Yangzhou
35 天目湖
Tianmu Lake, Liyang
36 宜兴张公洞
Cave of Revered Mr. Zhang, Yixing

35

36

浙江省
ZHEJIANG PROVINCE

浙江省简称浙，地处中国东南沿海，□□濒东海。全省面积10万多平方公□，□□4600多万，有汉、畲、回、满、苗等民族。省会杭州市。

浙江省以丘陵、山地为主，约占全省面积的70%，主要山脉有雁荡山、天目山、天台山、莫干山等。沿海岛屿星罗棋布，全省共有大小岛屿3000多个。

浙江省是著名的鱼米之乡和丝绸之府，也是中国旅游业最发达的地区之一。既富名山胜水，又多文物古迹，有"文物之都"的美誉。西湖、雁荡山、普陀山、□□湖、楠溪江、富春江、新安江、大□□、嵊泗列岛等均为国家重点风景名胜区，还有六和塔、保国寺、岳飞□、□来峰造像、天一阁等国家重点文物保护单位19处。主要旅游城市有杭州、宁波、□州、绍兴、舟山等。当地还有许多民俗节庆活动，如西湖国际游船节、国际钱塘江观潮节、普陀山朝圣等。

On the northeastern coast of China, Zhejiang Province faces the East Sea with the abbreviation of *Zhe*. The province has a territory of more than 100,000 square meters and a population of 46 million, including ethnic Han, She, Hui, Manchu, Miao, and others. Hangzhou is the capital city.

Mountains and hilly land make up roughly 70 per cent of the province's total area. Major mountains of the province are Yandang, Tianmu, Tiantai and Mogan. The offshore of Zhejiang is dotted with more than 3,000 islands in various sizes.

Reputed as the "Land of Fish and Rice" and "Home to Silk", Zhejiang is one of the most famous provinces of tourism. Also called as "the Capital of Cultural Relics", it is known for the se-renity and elegance of its landscape. National key scenic resorts in the province include West Lake, Yandang Mountain, Putuo Mountain, One-Thousand-Island Lake, Nanxijiang River, Fuchun and Xin'an rivers, Tiantai Mountain, Shengsi Islands, and so on. There are 19 sites under protection as key national cultural relics, such as Six-Harmony Pagoda, National Preservation Temple, Tomb of General Yue Fei, stone sculptures of the Feilai Peak, Tianyi Pavilion. Hangzhou, Ningbo, Shaoxing and Zhoushan are major tourist cities. Local tourist programs are focused on folklore, such as the International Boat Festival on the West Lake, the Festival to Watch the High Tide of the Qiantang River, and the Pilgrimage to the Putuo Mountain.

↑ 西湖
West Lake

2

2 西湖　位于杭州市西部，三面环山，湖区面积5.6平方公里，周长约15公里。整个湖区由苏堤和白堤分割为5个大小不等的水域，是中国著名的风景名胜区。西湖风光秀丽，景因时变，最著名的十景有：曲院风荷、平湖秋月、断桥残雪、柳浪闻莺、雷峰夕照、南屏晚钟、花港观鱼、苏堤春晓、双峰插云、三潭印月等。宋代大文豪苏轼曾赞誉："欲把西湖比西子，淡妆浓抹总相宜。"

West Lake　Surrounded on three sides by rolling wooded hills, the West Lake lies on west edge of Hangzhou and is one of the most beautiful sights in China. The lake has a total area of 5.6 square kilometers and circumference of 15 kilometers. Two dykes, the Sudi Causeway and the Baidi Causeway, spread in the lake and divided it into five parts. The beauty of the West Lake lies in a lingering charm that survives the charge of seasons throughout a year, of hours in a day, and of different weather. Tourists have named these as the ten most beautiful sights at the West Lake, namely Lotus in the Breeze at Crooked Courtyard, Autumn Moon on Calm Lake, Remaining Snow at Broken Bridge, Listening to Orioles Singing in the Willows, Sunset Glow over Leifeng Peak, Evening Bell at Nanping Hill, Viewing Fish at Flowers Harbour, Spring Dawn at Sudi Causeway, Twin Peaks Piercing the Clouds, and Three Pools Mirroring the Moon. Sushi, a famous poem of the Song Dynasty, once compared the lake to Xizi (Xishi), an unrivalled beauty of the Spring and Autumn Period.

3 平湖秋月
　Autumn Moon on Calm Lake

3

4 西湖之春
West Lake in Spring

5 杭州春色
  Spring Scenery of Hangzhou
6 杭州虎跑泉
  Tiger-Running Spring, Hangzhou
7 杭州孤山
  Gushan Hill, Hangzhou
8 杭州牡丹亭
  Peony Pavilion, Hangzhou

9

9 灵隐寺 坐落在杭州灵隐山脚下，由印度高僧慧理和尚创建于东晋咸和元年（公元326年）。现存主要建筑有天王殿、大雄宝殿、药师殿等。其中，大雄宝殿高33.6米，是中国最大的单层重檐建筑之一，内供释迦牟尼佛像高24.8米，用24块香樟木雕成。

Lingyin Temple   Located at the foot of Lingyin Mountain, Lingyin (Inspired Seclusion) Temple was first built by an Indian monk in 326 during the Eastern Jin Dynasty. On the compound's central axis stand the Hall of Heavenly Kings, the Shrine of Sakyamuni Buddha and the Hall of Bhaisajya. The Shrine of Sakyamuni Buddha with one story and double eaves is 33.6 meters in height, making it one of the tallest one-storey buildings in China. A statue of Sakyamuni, carved out of 24 pieces of camphor wood, stands 24.8 meters high in the hall.

10 杭州保俶塔
   Baochu Pagoda, Hangzhou
11 灵隐寺飞来峰
   Feilai Peak (Peak Flown from Afar)
12 杭州六和塔
   Six-Harmony Pagoda, Hangzhou
13 竹径
   Bamboo Path

14

14–16 普陀山　位于杭州湾以东约100海里的莲花洋中的海岛之上，是中国佛教四大名山之一，为观音菩萨的道场。海岛面积12.76平方公里，海拔约300米，素有"海天佛国"之称。主要胜迹有普济寺、法雨寺、潮音洞、梵音洞、千步沙、紫竹林等。

Putuo Mountain　Located on the Lotus Flowers Sea, about 100 sea miles east to the Hangzhou Bay, Putuo Mountain, regarded as the Buddhist Rites for Avalokitesvara Bodhisattva, is one of the four most famous Mountains of Buddhism. The island, covering an area of 12.76 square kilometers and rising about 300 meters above sea level, is reputed as the "Buddhist Kingdom on the Sea". Major attractions include Puji Temple, Fayu Temple, Chaoyin Cave, Fanyin Cave, Thousand-Pace Sands and Purple Bamboo Forest.

15

16

17

17、18 楠溪江　位于温州市永嘉县北，以
"水秀、岩奇、瀑多、村古"著称。楠溪江景观
丰富，有百丈瀑、陶公洞、石门台、十二峰等
景点。其中，陶公洞因南朝陶弘景得名，洞呈
螺壳状，宽敞而无曲折，被誉为道教"天下第
十二福地"。

Nanxijiang River　One of the national scenic
resorts, it is located north in Yongjia County,
Wenzhou City, and famous for beautiful water,
grotesque rocks, many waterfalls and ancient
villages. Major attractions include Hundred-
Zhang Waterfall, Cave of Revered Mr. Tao,
Stone-Gate Terrace, Twelve Peaks, and so on.
The Cave of Revered Mr. Tao derived its name
from Tao Hongjing (456-536), a noted thinker
of Taoism of the Southern Dynasty. The conch-
like cave is spacious and straight, and is
reputed as "the Number Twelve Auspicious
Land of the Taoism Under Heaven".

18

19

19 千岛湖　位于新安江上游，淳安县境内，是新安江水电站建成后形成的巨型人工湖。水域面积约580平方公里，有1078个大小岛屿，景色优美，特色各异。

Qiandaohu　Qiandaohu (One-Thousand-Island Lake) is located on the upper reaches of the Xin'an River in Chun'an County, which came into being with the completion of a dam for the Xin'an River Hydroelectric Power Station. The lake covers an area of more than 580 square meters, including 1,078 islands of different sizes and featuring beautiful scenery and distinct charactristics.

20 绍兴禹陵
Mausoleum of King Yu, Shaoxing
21 绍兴鉴湖
Jianhu Lake, Shaoxing

21

22、23 东湖 位于绍兴市东 3.5 公里处，以山清、水秀、石奇闻名，与杭州西湖、嘉兴南湖并称浙江省"三大名湖"。这里原为一座高约 60 米的小山，从汉代起在此凿山采石，千百年来，形成了深坑巨洞，积水成湖的景观。

East Lake   The lake is located in the east suburbs of Shaoxing, three kilometers from the city. Featuring an elegant landscape of lakes and mountains and fantastic stones, the East Lake is known as one of the Three Famous Lakes in Zhejiang Province, the other two being the West Lake in Hangzhou and the South Lake in Jiaxing. The East Lake used to be a hill about 60 meters in height. From the Han Dynasty, stone-men had been there to quarry stones. After thousand years of excavation, parts of the hill were hollowed, forming a unique scene of lake.

25

24 绍兴兰亭
Orchid Pavilion, Shaoxing
25 绍兴鹅池
Pond of Goose, Shaoxing

26 雁荡山风景区　位于东清县境内，总面积
4□□方公里，分为8个景区，共有500多个景
点□□奇峰怪石、飞瀑流泉、古洞奇穴，胜门险
嶂和山顶平湖被誉为雁荡山"五绝"胜景。风
景区尤以瀑布最为著名。其中大龙湫瀑布落差
达190余米，气势磅礴，堪称奇观。

Yandang Mountain Scenic Resort   Located
in Dongqing County, Yandang Mountain
covers an area of 450 square kilometers,
comprising of 8 scenic zones and more than
500 scenic spots. Grotesque peaks and rocks,
graceful waterfalls and springs, ancient caves,
natural precipitous stone gates, and clear lake
on the summit are famed as the Five
Marvelous Spectacles of the mountain. The
most famous of Yandang Mountain are
waterfalls. Perhaps no waterfall here is more
tremendous and majestic than the 190-meter-
high Dalongqiu Waterfall.

27-33 浙江古镇　浙北地区湖泊众多，水网密布，许多水乡小镇古风犹存。其中，著名的有南浔、乌镇、西塘等。这些古镇有着丰富的历史文化积淀，布局为江南典型的"小桥、流水、人家"式：以河成街，桥街相连，依河筑屋，呈现一派古朴、幽静的生活气息。

Ancient Towns of Zhejiang　North of Zhejiang is crisscrossed by rivers and studded with lakes. Scattered in the network of water are many ancient towns. Of them, Nanxun, Wuzhen and Xitang are the most famous ones. All these towns, similar in basic layout, have a wealth of ancient objects and scenes rich in historical and cultural connotations. They are described as "intersected by many rivers, with stone bridges spanning over the water lanes and linking up the households on either side of each stream" — a typical layout of "small bridges, flowing water and by-water residences" in the area south of the Yangtze.

34 天台山　位于天台县北 3.5 公里处，风光秀丽，景色优美。主峰华顶山海拔 1098 米。天台山为佛教天台宗的发祥地，也是日本佛教天台宗的祖庭。位于山麓的国清寺建于隋开皇十八年（公元 598 年），现存建筑为清代重修，著名文物有大雄宝殿内明代 7 米高的铜铸释迦牟尼佛、王羲之鹅字碑等。

Tiantai Mountain　3.5 kilometers from Tiantai County, the mountain is famous for its beautiful scenery. The main peak of Huadingshan, is 1,098 meters above sea level. Tiantai Mountain is noted as the home to Chinese and Japanese followers of the Tiantai Sect of Buddhism. The Guoqing Monastery on the slopes of the mountain was built in 598 in the Sui Dynasty. Famous cultural relics are seven-meter-high bronze statue of Sakyamuni Buddha of the Ming Dynasty in the Shrine of Greatness and Magnificence, the tablet with the inscription of "E" (goose) by Wang Xizhi, a noted calligrapher of the Eastern Jin Dynasty, and so on.

35 宁波阿育王寺
Asoka Temple, Ningbo
36 柯岩石佛
Giant Stone Buddha of Keyan
37 宁波天童寺
Temple of Heavenly Virgin Boy, Ningbo
38 乡村春色
A view of the country in Zhejiang

安徽省
ANHUI PROVINCE

安徽省位于华东西北部，地跨长江、淮河。因境内有皖山（天柱山）、皖水，春秋时有皖国，故简称皖。全省面积近14万平方公里，人口5900多万，有汉、回、畲等民族。省会合肥市。

安徽省历史文化悠久，山川秀丽多姿，旅游资源丰富。主要风景名胜区有世界文化与自然双重遗产黄山风景区，中国佛教四大名山之一九华山，四大道教名山之一齐云山，以及天柱山、大别山等。寿县、亳州、歙县为中国历史文化名城。宣城、徽州、亳州是文房四宝的主要生产基地。皖南黟县保留的明、清民居建筑被联合国教科文组织列为世界文化遗产。其他名胜古迹还有采石矶、巢湖、小孤山、太平湖等。黄梅戏和花鼓也源于安徽省。

Anhui Province spans the basins of the Yangtze and Huaihe rivers in the northwestern part of east China. It is abbreviated as "*Wan*", because of the Wan Mountain (present Tianzhu Mountain), Wanhe River in its territory and the State of Wan, which existed during the Spring and Autumn Period. The province with an area of almost 140,000 square kilometers has a population of 59 million people of Han, Hui, She and others ethnic backgrounds. The provincial capital is Hefei.

Having a long history and pageant culture, Anhui abounds in resources of tourism and is famed for its statuesque mountains and ribbon-like rivers. Major scenic resorts include Mount Huangshan, a world cultural and natural heritage site, Mount Jiuhua, one of China's four most famous Buddhist mountains, Mount Qiyun, one of the four Taoist mountain sanctuaries, as well as Tianzhu and Dabie mountains. Shouxian, Bozhou and Shexian are famous historical and cultural cities in China. The dwellings in Yixian County are reminiscent of Ming and Qing architecture, which are on the World Heritage List. Anhui is also a major center for production of the "four treasures of the study". Other tourist spots include: Caishiji, Chaohu Lake, Mount Xiaogu and Taiping Lake.

1 黄山雪景
Mount Huangshan after snow

2

2-6 黄山　位于安徽省南部，是中国十大风
景名胜区之一，风光奇丽，景色如画，自古即
为旅游胜地，有"黄山归来不看岳"之说，尤
以"奇松、怪石、云海、温泉"四绝而享有盛
名。黄山历史文化丰厚，文物古迹众多。1990
年，黄山风景名胜区被联合国教科文组织列为
自然与文化双重遗产。主要景区有莲花峰、光
明顶、天都峰、西海、清凉台等。

Mount Huangshan　Situated in the southern
part of Anhui Province, Mount Huangshan is
one of the top ten tourist attractions and

3

安
徽

4

destinations in China. Since it boasts of combining the characters of many famous mountains in China, there goes a saying: "Having seen the all-inclusive Mount Huangshan, one does not wish to see any of the five major mountains." Mount Huangshan owns its unique scenic value to four major factors: oddly shaped pines, grotesque rocks, clouds sea, and hot spring. The remains of long history and rich culture of the mountain could be found here and there. In 1990, the UNESCO put the Mount Huangshan on its List of World Heritage. Main scenic areas of Mount Huangshan include Lianhua Peak, Guangmingding Peak, Tiandu Peak, West Sea, Cool Terrace, and so on.

6

中国风景名胜

7

7-9 安徽古村落　2000 年，坐落在皖南黟县的西递村和宏村被联合国教科文组织列入《世界遗产名录》。西递村始建于公元 11 世纪，现保存有明、清古民居 124 幢，祠堂 3 幢，牌楼 1 座，具有典型的明、清建筑风格。宏村被誉为"中国画里的乡村"。现存明、清古建筑 137 幢，其中承志堂、敬修堂被称为"民间故宫"。

Ancient Villages in Anhui Province　Both in Yixian County, Xidi and Hongcun villages were inscribed on the UNESCO's List of World Heritage in 2000. Named as "the Museum of Ming and Qing Residential Buildings", Xidi Village was firstly constructed in the 11th century. There exist 124 ancient residential buildings, 3 clan temples and 1 memorial arch, which have the Ming and Qing styles. Hongcun Village, reputed as "the Village in Traditional Chinese Painting", has 137 ancient buildings. Among them, the halls of Chengzhi and Jingxiu are famed as "the Local Palace Museum".

8

9

10

10 古牌坊群　位于歙县西 6 公里处的棠越村，共有 7 座，为鲍氏家族所建，其中 3 座建于明朝，余下 4 座为清代建筑。牌坊古朴雄伟，雕刻精细，是典型徽派石雕。

The Complex of Seven Arches　Built by Bao Clan, it is located in Tangyue Village, 6 kilometers west of Shexian County. Three of the seven arches were built during the Ming Dynasty, and the other four were built during the Qing Dynasty. These memorial arches wind their ways into a simple and elegant group, and they are outstanding stone carving of Hui school.

11

11-13 九华山 位于青阳县西南 20 公里处，是地藏王菩萨的道场，为中国佛教四大名山之一。景区面积120平方公里，有大小山峰99座。九华山拥有奇峰怪石，飞瀑流泉，享有"东南第一山"之誉。现存化城寺、肉身宝殿、甘露寺等 78 座寺庙。

Mt. Jiuhua   The mountain lies 20 kilometers southwest of Qingyang County. As the Bodhimanda of Ksitigarbha Bodhisattva, it is regarded as one of the four most famous Buddhist Mountains. It consists of 99 peaks. The 120-square-kilometer area is full of ridges and peaks, exotic-shaped rocks, roaring waterfalls and clear streams, which establish a reputation of "Number one mountain in the Southeast China." 78 temples are preserved to this day, and the Huacheng Temple, Corporeal Body Hall and Temple of Nectar are the most famous.

12

13

福建省
FUJIAN PROVINCE

福建省简称闽，位于中国东南沿海，与台湾省隔海相望，是中国对外交流的窗口之一，也是台胞的"祖家"和著名的侨乡。全省面积12万多平方公里，其中，约80%为丘陵、山地，有"东南山国"之称。福建省人口3400多万，主要有▮▮、回、蒙古、苗、壮、高山等民族。省会福州市。

福建省历史悠久，旅游资源丰富，以山清水绿、风景秀丽而闻名。全省主要风景名胜40多处，重点文物保护单位40余处。武夷山被联合国教科文组织列入《世界遗产名录》。国家重点风景名胜区有太姥山、清源山、鼓浪屿、万石山等，主要名胜古迹有涌泉寺、南山寺、广化寺、开元寺、南普陀寺、洛阳桥等。

Fujian (*Min* for Short), a coastal province in southeast China facing Taiwan across the Straits, is one of windows for China's exchanges with the outside world, and home to numerous Chinese residing abroad and most of the Taiwan compatriots. Covering an area of 120,000 square kilometers, the province is reputed as a "Mountain Kingdom of Southeast China", because a series of mountains and hilly lands make up 80 per cent of its total territory. It has a population of 34 million including Hans, Shes, Huis, Mongolians, Miaos, Zhuangs, Gaoshans, and so on. Fuzhou City is the capital of Fujian Province.

The province's long history and rich tourist resources are set off splendidly by lush-vegetation-covered mountains and crystal clear waters. There are more than 40 main scenic spots in the provinces, and 40-odd sites under protection as key cultural relics. The Mount Wuyi is a UNESCO world natural and cultural heritage site. National scenic resorts include Taimu Mountain, Qingyuan Mountain, Gulangyu Island, Wanshi Mountain, and so on. Main sites of historical and cultural interest include Yongquan Temple, Nanshan Temple, Guanghua Temple, Kaiyuan Temple, Nanputuo Temple, and Luoyang Bridge.

1 武夷山
Mount Wuyi

福建省

2-4 武夷山█位于福建省北部，以丹霞地貌为主，山清水秀，溪谷环绕，自然风光优美，历史悠久，文化遗存众多。主要景观有九曲溪，36峰和99岩等。武夷山也是世界动植物种类最为丰富的地区之一，素有"昆虫世界"、"鸟类天堂"和"蛇的王国"之称。1999年，武夷山被联合国教科文组织列入《世界遗产名录》。

Mount Wuyi   The Mountain is located in the north of Fujian Province. Possessing a well-preserved ecological environment on a danxia landform, it is not only famous for its pictur-esque scenery — beautiful mountains, vigorous rocks, limpid waters, but also its centuries-old cultures. Main attractions include Jiuqu (Nine-Crooked) Stream, 36 peaks, 99 rocks, and so on. Every scenic spot is unique and fabulous. Mount Wuyi Preserve is also a paradise for the wild animals and plants. People call the "world of insects","heaven of birds" and kingdom of snakes". In 1999, UNESCO inscribed the Mount Wuyi on the List of World Heritage.

6 福州森林公园大榕树
Banyan King in Fuzhou Forest Park

5 鼓山   位于福州市东郊17公里处，海拔969米。全山以涌泉寺为中心，山上景色清幽。涌泉寺兴建于五代后梁开平二年（公元908年），有"闽刹之冠"的美誉。从山麓至寺院，有一条古老石径，共有石磴2500多级，两侧劲松碧翠，幽涧流泉，有回龙阁、放生池、香炉峰等50余景。

Drum Mountain   Located 17 kilometers east from Fuzhou, the beautiful and secluded Drum Mountain with an elevation of 969 meters above sea level is centered by the Yongquan (Bubbling Spring) Temple. The temple built in 908, or the second year of the Later Liang's Kaiping reign during the Five Dynasties, is reputed as "the Number One of All Temples in Fujian". An ancient stone path with more than 2,500 steps stretches along the slopes of the mountain to the temple. On both side of the path are luxuriant cypresses and pine trees, secluded streams and flowing springs. There are 50-odd scenic spots, such as Huilong Pavilion, Fangsheng Pond and Incense Burner Peak.

7 鼓浪屿 位于厦门市西南，是一个面积约1.8平方公里的小岛。岛上繁花似锦，绿树成荫，风光秀丽，有"海上花园"之誉。日光岩为全岛最高点，登顶可俯瞰厦门全景。菽庄花园设计精巧，曲桥假山，山亭古洞，相映成趣。

Gulangyu Island   Covering an area of almost 1.8 square kilometers, Gulanyu Island is situated in the southwest of Xiamen proper. The blooming flowers, flourish trees and beautiful scenery win her a name of "Garden on the Sea". The Sunlight Rock, the highest point on the island, offers you a panoramic view of the sea and the city. Shuzhuang Garden is elaborately designed with artificial rocks, zigzagging bridges, beautiful pavilions and ancient caves, all setting off harmoniously.

8 厦门南普陀寺 位于厦门市东南，为闽南著名古刹。寺庙始建于唐代，坐北朝南，占地约3万平方米，主要建筑有天王殿、大雄宝殿、大悲殿、藏经阁等。

Nanputuo Temple   On the southeastern outskirts of Xiamen City is the Buddhist Temple called Nanputuo. The famous ancient temple was first built during the Tang Dynasty. It covers 30,000 square meters with four main buildings — Hall of Heavenly Kings, Shrine of Greatness and Magnificence, Hall of Great Compassion, and Sutra-Keeping Pavilion — on the north-south axis.

9-12 集美 位于厦门市区北，三面环海，是爱国华侨陈嘉庚先生的故乡。陈嘉庚先生曾在此办学，兴建了█新学校，包括厦门大学，以及科学馆、体育馆、图书馆、医院、美术馆和航海俱乐部等，因此小镇又被称为"集美学村"。陈先生的墓地——鳌园也建于此。其他景点有归来堂、陈嘉庚故居、延平故垒等。

Jimei   Facing the sea in three sides, Jimei lies to the north of Xiamen proper, where is the hometown of Mr. Tan Kah-Kee(1874-1961), a famous overseas Chinese lead who devoted himself wholly to education. Mr. Tan built 12 different kinds of schools including Xiamen University, science center, gymnasium, library, hospital, art gallery, navigation club, and so on, hence the town was also called █imei Acadamic Village". Mr. Tan's graveyard, the Turtle Garden, lies in the southeast of the town. Other attractions include Returness Garden, former residence of Mr. Tan Kah-Kee, and Yanping Ancient Fortress.

11

12

13 泉州惠安石雕
   Stone carving of Huian, Quanzhou
14 泉州德化岱仙瀑
   Daixian Waterfalls in Dehua, Quanzhou
15 泉州清源山老君岩
   Rock of Lao Tzu on Qingyuan Mountain,
   Quanzhou
16 泉州开元寺石塔
   Stone pagoda in Kaiyuan Temple, Quanzhou
17 泉州开元寺
   Kaiyuan Temple, Quanzhou

江西省
JIANGXI PROVINCE

江西省位于长江中下游南岸，因赣江为其境内第一大河，故简称赣。全省面积 16 万多平方公里，人口 4140 万，有汉、回、苗、畲、瑶等民族。省会南昌市。

江西省东、南、西三面有武夷、南岭、罗霄等山岭环绕，中部多丘陵，山地占全省面积64％，北部为鄱阳湖平原。

江西省历史悠久，古称"文献之邦"，人杰地灵，许多历史名人均出于此，有陶渊明、欧阳修、朱熹、文天祥、汤显祖、宋应星等。江西又富山水之胜，著名旅游景区有世界遗产庐山风景名胜区，道教名山龙虎山、三清山、"革命摇篮"井冈山和鄱阳湖自然风景区；名胜古迹有滕王阁、浔阳楼、能仁寺、烟水亭、白鹿洞书院等，主要旅游城市有南昌、九江、"瓷都"景德镇、赣州、吉安等。

Located on the southern bank of the lower reaches of the Yangtze, Jiangxi is called *Gan* for short, because of the Ganjiang River, the largest in the province. It has a total area of more than 160,000 square kilometers, and a population of 41.40 million consisting of ethnic peoples such as Han, Hui, Miao, She and Yao. Nanchang is the provincial capital.

Mountains of Wuyi, Nanling and Luoxiao surround Jiangxi in three sides of east, south and west, and hilly land covers the middle of the province, which make up 64 per cent of its total territory. The northern part is the Poyang Lake Plain.

Jiangxi has a long history, famed as "the Land of Literature" since ancient times, and it is home to numerous famed cultural personage, including Tao Yuanming, Ouyang Xiu, Zhu Xi, Wen Tianxiang, Tang Xianzu, Song Yingxing, and so on. And also, Jiangxi is rich in scenery with mountains and rivers. Famous tourist scenic areas include world heritage site — Mount Lushan, Taoist famous mountains — Longhu and Sanqing, "Cradle of the Revolution" — Jinggang Mountain, Poyang Lake Nature Reserve, etc. Sites of historical and cultural interest include Tengwang Pavilion, Xunyang Tower, Nengren Temple, Yanshui Pavilion, Academy of White Deer Cave, and so on. Nanchang, Jiujiang, "Porcelain Capital" — Jingdezhen, Ganzhou and Ji'an are major tourist cities.

1 庐山
Mount Lushan

2 庐山　位于江西省北部，北临长江，东濒中国最大的淡水湖——鄱阳湖。庐山拥有雄奇的山峰，变幻的云海，神奇的飞瀑和历史悠久的文物古迹，是中国风景名山之一和著名的避暑胜地。由99座山峰组成，主峰大汉阳峰海拔1474米。主要风景名胜点有五老峰、三叠泉、含鄱口、三宝树、龙首崖、花径、东林寺等。1996年，庐山被联合国教科文组织列入《世界遗产名录》。

Mount Lushan   Located in the northern part of Jiangxi Province, Mount Lushan faces the Yangtze River to the north and borders on the east with Poyang Lake, the largest fresh water lake in China. The mountain consists of 99 peaks, the tallest being Dahanyang, rising to the height of 1,474 meters above sea level. With fantastic blend of imposing and magnificent peaks, changing sea of clouds, spectacular waterfalls and time-honored cultural relics, it is one of the most famous mountains and summer resorts in China, and was inscribed on the World Heritage List by the UNESCO in 1996. Main scenic spots include the Peak of Five Old Men, Three-Tier Spring, Hanpokou Pass, Three Treasure Trees, Dragon-Head Cliff, Flower Path, Donglin Monastery,and so on.

3 庐山仙人洞
　　Immortal's Cave of Mount Lushan

4

4 庐山龙首崖云海
　Clouds Sea at Dragon-Head Cliff,
　Mount Lushan

5 三叠泉　位于庐山以东的九叠谷中，瀑布从五老峰奔泻而下，依山势分为上、中、下三级，落差150余米，被誉为"庐山第一奇观"，有"未到三叠泉，不算庐山客"之说。

Three-Tier Spring　Situated in Jiudie Valley, east of Mount Lushan, Three-Tier Spring is the most outstanding water attraction of the mountain. This waterfall plummets more than 150 meters from the pinnacle of the Peak of Five-Old-Men, having three tiers. It is reputed as "the Number One Spectacular View of Mt. Lushan". A famous saying goes "He who hasn't been to the Three-Tier Spring is not a real visitor to the Mount Lushan".

5

6、7 白鹿洞书院　位于五老峰南麓，是中国最早的高等学府之一。唐贞元元年（公元785年），李渤、李涉兄弟在此隐居创建，因饲养一只白鹿而得名。

Academy of White Deer Cave　Located on the south slopes of the Peak of Five-Old-Men, the academy is one of the oldest institutions for high learning in China. It was built in 785, or the first year of Tang Zhenyuan's reign by the brothers of Li Bo and Li She. It was so-called because one of founders once raised a pet white deer.

7

8 九江琵琶亭
  Pipa Pavilion, Jiujiang
9 九江浔阳楼
  Xunyang Tower, Jiujiang
10 九江烟水亭
  Yanshui (Misty Water) Pavilion, Jiujiang

11 滕王阁 □ 立于南昌市西长江边，是中国古代四大名楼之一。初建于唐永徽四年（公元653年）。由唐太宗李世民之弟、滕王李元婴督造，因而得名。后因王勃所著《滕王阁序》而名扬天下。滕王阁在历史上屡毁屡修，1926年被焚毁，现存建筑为1989年仿宋代建筑风格重修，阁高57.5米，上下九层，辉煌壮丽。

Tengwang Pavilion   Located on the bank of the Yangtze River, west of Nanchang, it is one of the Four Most Famous Pavilions in ancient China. The pavilion was first built in 653, or the fourth year during the reign of Yonghui, when Li Yuanying (King Teng), a younger brother of Emperor Taizong of the Tang Dynasty, was the governor of Nanchang, thus the name of the building. The reputation of Tengwang Pavilion, to a great extent, is due to a well-known prose — "Preface to Tengwang Pavilion" by Wang Bo, a reputable poet of the dynasty. It was destroyed and rebuilt many times in history, until it was burned to ashes in 1926. In 1989, the pavilion was rebuilt according to the style of architecture in the Song Dynasty. The present nine-storied building stands 57.5 meters high, and looks quite magnificent and splendid.

12 景德镇
A view of Jingdezhen,
the Porcelain Capital
13 制陶
Making Porcelains
14 景德镇瓷器
Jingdezhen Porcelains

15 石钟山　位于湖口县鄱阳湖出口处，海拔不足70米，因山石多隙，水石相博，发出钟鸣般的声响，因此得名。苏轼曾写有著名的《石钟山记》一文。由于地势险要，这里为兵家必争之地。远在三国时，东吴大将周瑜就在这一带湖中操练水军；清朝时，太平军曾在这里大败曾国藩水师。

Stone Bell Hill　Situated at the mouth of Poyang Lake by Hukou County, the Stone Bell Hill is no more that 70 meters in height. Water of the lake, lapping into the cracks and crannies around the base, produces a bell-like sound hence the name. Su Shi, a noted literati once wrote the famous article of "The Notes of Stone Bell Hill". It was also a military strategic spot in ancient time. Zhou Yu, a famous general of the Eastern Wu during the Three Kingdoms drilled the navy on the Lake here; and the Taiping Rebel once defeated Qing armies leaded by Zeng Guofan here.

17 瑞金革命遗址
Revolutionary Site in Ruijin
18 湖口鞋山
Shoe Hill in Hukou County, Jiujiang

16 龙虎山　位于贵溪县西，属武夷山余脉，具有典型的丹霞地貌特征，山清水秀，文物丰富，是中国道教正一派的发源地。山上主要道教建筑有上清宫、天师府等。在仙水岩陡峭的石壁上，保留有2600多年前春秋战国时期的崖墓百余座，堪称奇观。山东部还有南宋大理学家陆九渊创建的"象山书院"遗址。

Longhu Mountain　Located west to Guixi County, the Longhu (Dragon and Tiger) Mountain having a typical danxia landform belongs to the Wuyi Mountains range. It is noted for lush-vegetation-covered peaks, graceful rivers and abundant cultural relics. As the birthplace of the Zhengyi Sect of the Taoism, the mountain is dotted with Taoist buildings including Shangqing Palace, Tianshi Mansion mainly. More than a hundred coffins are seen suspended on the cliffs of Xianshui Rock, which could date back to 2600 years ago during the Spring and Autumn and the Warring States periods. Situated on the eastern part of the mountain are the ruins of "Xiangshan Academy", which was established by Lu Jiuyuan, a celebrated scholar of Confucianism.

19

19、20 婺源风光
Beautiful scenery of Wuyuan
21、22 流坑古村
Liukeng, an ancient village

20

21

22

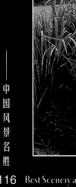

23 井冈山 位于江西省西南，湘赣交界处的罗霄山脉中段，总面积660多平方公里，最高处海拔1841米。井冈山风景秀丽，是闻名中外的革命根据地，保存有多处革命胜迹，主要有井冈山革命博物馆、大小等五井、黄洋界哨口等。

Jinggang Mountains Located in southwest Jiangxi and the middle part of Luoxiao Mountains where Hunan and Jiangxi provinces meet, the Jinggang Mountains covers an area of more than 660 square kilometers. With an altitude of 1,841 meters, the mountains look majestic and graceful. So many revolutionary sites, monuments, and museums indicate that Jinggang Mountains was a cradle of Chinese revolution. Major revolutionary sites are Jinggang Mountain Revolutionary Museum, five villages of Great Well, Lesser Well, Upper Well, Middle Well and Lower Well, Huang-yangjie Post, and so on.

24 三清山
A picturesque scene of Sanqing
(Pure Trinity) Mountain

山东省

SHANDONG PROVINCE

山东省简称鲁，位于黄河中下游，因地处太行山以东而得名。春秋时期为齐、鲁国地，故山东又称为"齐鲁"。全省面积15万多平方公里，人口9000多万，有汉、回、满、蒙古、壮等民族。省会济南市。

山东省是中国古代灿烂文化的发祥地之一。早在原始社会时期，山东就有人类生存和繁衍，并创造了著名的大汶口文化和龙山文化。山东也是孔子和孟子的家乡。

山东省旅游资源丰富。泰山风景区、孔庙、孔府、孔林已被联合国教科文组织列入《世界遗产名录》。青岛、烟台、威海、蓬莱等均为著名的海滨旅游胜地。其他风景名胜有济南大明湖、千佛山，青岛栈桥、崂山，蓬莱市蓬莱阁、潍坊风筝博物馆，淄博齐故城遗址、蒲松龄故居，邹城孟府等。

Lu is abbreviation for Shandong, a province in the lower reaches of the Yellow River. The present name comes from its location east to Taihang Mountain. During the Spring and Autumn and Warring States periods, most part of Shandong belonged to the states of Qi and Lu, so it also called Qilu by later people. Over 150,000 square kilometers in area, Shandong has a population of more than 90 million people including Hans, Huis, Manchurians, Mongolians, Zhuangs and other ethnic peoples. Jinan is the provincial capital.

Shandong was one of the birthplaces of the glorious culture of ancient China. Early in the Primitive Society, people lived there and created the famous Dawenkou and Longshan cultures about 4,000 years ago. It was also the homeland of Confucius and Mencius, two celebrated thinkers of ancient China.

The province abounds in tourist resources. Mount Taishan, and Temple, Mansion and Cemetery of Confucius are all on the UNESCO's World Heritage List. Qingdao, Yantai, Penglai, Weihai are famous seaside resorts. Other scenic spots and historical and cultural sites include Daming Lake and Thousand-Buddha Mountain in Jinan, Plank Pathway and Mount Laoshan in Qingdao, Penglai Pavilion of Penglai City, Kite Museum of Weifang, ruins of ancient city of Qi State and former residence of Pu Songling, author of *The Strange Stories from a Lonely Studio*, in Zibo, and Mencius Masion in Zoucheng City.

1 曲阜孔庙
Confucius Temple, Qufu

2-5 曲阜三孔　孔庙、孔府、孔林位于中国历史文化名城、孔子的故里曲阜，于1994年，被联合国教科文组织列入《世界遗产名录》。孔庙，初建于公元前478年，是祭祀孔子的庙宇。占地22万平方米，有各类房舍466间，为中国最大的文庙。主要建筑有大成殿、杏坛、奎文阁、圣迹殿等。其中，大成殿，面积1836平方米，是中国三大殿之一。圣迹殿为保存《圣迹图》而建。《圣迹图》生动地讲述了孔子一生的主要经历。孔府，位于孔庙之东，为孔子后代长子长孙的居位之所，有房屋463间，是中国规模最大的宗族府弟之一。孔林，是孔子及其后裔的墓地，占地约200万平方米，为中国规模最大、持续年代最长的宗族墓群。

Temple, Mansion and Cemetery of Confucius in Qufu　Located in Qufu, one of the national famous historical and cultural cities and hometown of Confucius, the Confucius Temple, Mansions and Graveyard were inscribed on the World Heritage List by the UNESCO in 1994. First built in 478 BC in memory of the great philosopher and founder of Confucianism, Confucius Temple covers an area of 22 hectares and has 466 rooms, making it the largest of its kind in China. Among the principal structures in the temple are Dachengdian (Hall of Great Achievements), Apricot Rostrum Pavilion, Kuiwen Pavilion, Shengjidian (Hall of Holy Remains), and so on. Dacheng Hall, having a total of 1,836 square meters, is one of the Three Grand Halls in China. Shengjidian houses a series of engraved stones, telling stories of the philosopher. To the east of the Confucius Temple, the aristocratic Confucius Mansion used to be the residence of descen-dants of Confucius — the Kongs. Containing 463 buildings, the complex is one of the largest and finest of its kind in China. The Confucius Cemetery is the largest and oldest family cemetery in the country, and covers about 200 hectares.

5

6-8 泰山 古称岱宗、岱山，位于山东省中部，南起泰安市，北至济南市郊。风景区总面积125平方公里，最高峰玉皇顶海拔1545米。泰山以雄伟壮丽著称，自然风光优美，是天然的历史、艺术博物馆。云海和日出是其两大自然奇观。泰山为五岳之东岳，文物古迹众多。因历代帝王登基之初，多来泰山举行封禅大典，祭告天地，而享有"五岳独尊"之美誉。1987年，泰山被联合国教科文组织列入《世界遗产名录》。山上主要景点60余处，主要有岱庙、中天门、南天门、碧霞祠、玉皇顶、五大夫松等。

Mount Taishan Located at the central part of Shandong Province and lying across Taian and Jinan, Mount Taishan, the East Sacred Mountain, was called Daizong or Daishan in ancient times. Covering an area of 125 square kilometers and with a height of 1,545 meters, it is famous for its intense grandeur and beautiful natural scenery, and also has a reputation of "a Natural Museum of History and Art" for its countless cultural relics and historical sites. The most spectacular features of the mountain are enjoying cloud-sea and sun rising. As the royal object of cult, Mount Taishan was the venue where past emperors of various dynasties used to worship Heaven and Earth, and was thought to be the most famed among the Five Sacred Mountains in China. In 1987, it became a world heritage site of culture and nature. Atop the mountain are more than 60 main scenic spots including the Dai Temple, Mid-Heaven Gate, South-Heaven Gate, Bixia Temple, Jade Emperor Summit, and Five-Dafu Pines.

9　济南大明湖
　　Daming Lake, Jinan
10、11　长岛风光
　　Scenery of Changdao
　　(Long Island)
12　青岛栈桥
　　Plank Pathway, Qingdao

13

14

the background of history and culture in modern times. Among the major scenic spots and historical monuments are Zhanqiao (Plank Pathway), Lesser Qingdao, Xiaoyushan Park, Eight Major Passes, Laoshan Mountain Scenic Area and Shilaoren National Holiday Resort.

15 崂山风景区

Laoshan Mountain Scenic Zone, Qingdao

13、14 青岛市　位于胶东半岛、胶州湾畔，三面环海，气候宜人，是中国著名的海滨避暑度假胜地和国家历史文化名城，面积 1 万多平方公里，人口 703 万。优美的自然景观和丰富的近代历史文化内涵构成了青岛旅游的基本特征。主要名胜古迹有：栈桥、小青岛、小鱼山公园、八大关、崂山风景区、石老人国家旅游度假区等。

Qingdao　Qingdao is a well-known seaside resort and a famous historical and cultural city. Located on the Jiaodong Peninsula and by the Bay of Jiaozhou, the city is surrounded by the sea on three sides and enjoys a congenial climate. The basic features of Qingdao as a tourist attraction are that with the sea as the main theme. The sea, the mountains and the city form a picture of natural scenery against

15

16

17

16 烟台海滨
　　A seaside view of Yantai

17 蓬莱阁　位于蓬莱市北1公里的丹崖山巅。传闻秦始皇和汉武帝曾登临此处求长生不老之药；民间传说＂八仙＂亦是在此处过海。阁楼始建于北宋嘉佑六年（公元1061年）。整个规模宏大的古建筑群由蓬莱阁、天后宫、龙五宫、吕祖殿、三清殿、弥陀寺六大单体及其附属建筑组成，占地面积3.28万平方米。阁内文人墨宝、楹联石刻，不胜枚举。

Penglai Pavilion　Sitting on summit of Danya Mountain and 1 kilometer north of the city of same name, the magnificent Penglai Pavilion was first built in 1061. Legend has it that Emperor Qin Shihuang and Emperor Wu of the Han Dynasty once sought for the elixir of life here. The famous legend of "Eight Immortals Crossing the Sea" finds its origin here. It is a vast group of ancient buildings on a land of 32,800 square meters, composed of the six buildings and their attached constructions: Penglai Pavilion, Tianhou and Longwu palaces, Luzu and Sanqing halls and Mituo Temple. Attractively on display in these buildings are works of calligraphy of famous literary writers, couplet hung on the columns and stone inscriptions.

河南省
HENAN PROVINCE

河南省简称豫，位于黄河中下游、华中地区，向有"中原"、"中州"之称。全省总面积16万多平方公里，人口9256万，有汉、回、蒙、满、壮等41个民族，省会郑州市。

河南省地势西高东低，平原、山区面积各占一半。西北角三面环山，主要山脉有伏牛山、太行山、桐柏山、大别山和中岳嵩山，主要河流有黄河、淮河和卫河。

河南省历史悠久，有"中华民族摇篮"、"中原文化发祥地"之称，名胜古迹众多，历史文物极为丰富。洛阳、开封、安阳、南阳、商丘、郑州和浚县均被列为国家历史文化名城。主要名胜古迹及文化遗址有：世界文化遗产洛阳龙门石窟，包含仰韶、龙山和周文化的郑州大河村遗址，安阳殷墟，洛阳白马寺、关林，开封铁塔、相国寺、龙亭，登丰少林寺，嵩山风景名胜区等。

Situated in central China and the middle and lower reaches of the Yellow River, Henan Province abbreviated as "Yu" is also known as *Zhongzhou* or *Zhongyuan*, both meaning the central area. With an area of 160,000 square kilometers, Henan has a population of 92.56 million, which consists of 41 ethnic peoples including Hans, Huis, Mongolians, Manchurians and others. Zhengzhou is provincial capital.

Topographically, Henan slopes down from west to east; plain areas accounts for a half of the whole territory of the province, and mountain covers the rest. Northwestern Henan is screened by mountains on three sides. Major mountains of the province are Funiu, Taihang, Tongbai, Dabie and the Central Sacred Mountain — Mount Songshan.

Main rivers include the Yellow, Huaihe and Weihe rivers.

Having a long history, Henan is known as a "cradle of the Chinese civilization" and "birthplace of the culture of Central Plains". The province has numerous places of historical interest and scenic beauty, and abounds in cultural relics. Luoyang, Kaifeng, Anyang, Nanyang, Shangqiu, Zhengzhou and Junxian are all national famous historical and cultural cities. Major tourist attractions are: Longmen Grottoes, a world cultural heritage site, Dahe Village Ruins including Yangshao, Longshan and Zhou cultures, Yin Ruins, White-Horse Temple, Guanlin, Iron Pagoda, Grand Chancellor's Temple, Dragon Pavilion, Shaolin Temple and Mount Songshan Scenic Resort.

1 龙门石窟
Longmen Grottoes

2-4 龙门石窟　位于洛阳市南郊伊河两岸的山崖上。石窟始建于北魏年间，历经400余年大规模营造，其中，以北魏和唐代工程最为突出。东、西两山现存窟龛2100多个，造像10万余尊，碑刻题记3600多块，佛塔40余座。2000年，龙门石窟被联合国教科文组织列入《世界遗产名录》。

Longmen Grottoes　　Located in the south suburbs of Luoyang City, the Longmen Grottoes houses over 2,100 Buddhist niches, more than 100,000 sculptures, about 3,600 inscriptions and 40 Buddhist pagodas. They scatter on the eastern and western cliffs on both of the Yihe River. The construction of the Grottoes began during the period of Northern Wei (386-534), and had lasted for over 400 years. It was inscribed on the List of World Heritage by the UNESCO in 2000.

5 少林寺　位于登峰西北14公里处，少室山北麓，始建于北魏太和十九年（公元495年）。寺院共七进院落，占地面积约3万余平方米，气势宏伟，有█天下第一名刹█称。其中，千佛殿（又称毗卢阁）为寺内现存规模最大、保存最完整的古建，殿内有明代铜像、玉石像、壁画等文物。寺西300米处有始建于唐贞元七年（公元791年）的塔林，共有唐至清代砖石墓塔240余座，大小不一，形式各异，是少林寺历代和尚的墓地，为中国最大一处墓塔群。

Shaolin Temple　14 kilometers northwest from Dengfeng City and on the slopes of Shaoshi Mountain, the Shaolin Temple was first built in 495 during the Northern Wei Dynasty. The imposing temple consists of seven courtyards with a total of more than 30,000 square meters, and is reputed as "the Number One Famous Temple Under Heaven". The Hall of A-Thousand-Buddha, or the Shrine of Vairocana, one of the largest and best-preserved buildings of the temple, houses the bronze statue, jade statues and murals of the Ming Dynasty. To the west of the temple is a forest of 243 brick-and-masonry stupas of different sizes and architectural styles, built during a 1,000-year spanning from the Tang to Qing dynasties. It is the graveyard of monks of the temple, and is the largest group of tomb-pagoda in China.

6　少林寺塔林
Stupa Forest in Shaolin Temple
7　少林寺壁画
Murals in Shaolin Temple

8 嵩岳寺塔
Pagoda of Songyue Temple

9

9 白马寺　位于洛阳市东北12公里处。寺院始建于东汉永平十一年（公元68年），为中国最早的佛教寺院，在中国佛教史上占有重要地位。据说，印度高僧摄摩腾和竺法兰以白马驮经来洛阳传经，因此得名。白马寺建筑面积近4万平方米，由百余间殿堂组成，现存建筑为明清重修。大门外两匹石马为宋代雕刻。

White House Temple　One of the most venerable Buddhist shrines in China, the White House Temple stands 12 kilometers northeast of Luoyang. The present Ming and Qing buildings in the temple were built on the site of the original temple, which dated back 2000 years in 68 AD. The temple was the first Buddhist temple to be built in China and plays important role in the country's Buddhist history. Legend has it that two Buddhist monks from India, riding a white house, delivered the Buddhist scriptures to Luoyang — hence the name of the temple. Covering an area of almost 40,000 square meters, the temple consists of over a hundred halls and rooms.

10 登峰中岳庙
Temple of the Central Sacred Mountain,
Dengfeng
11 郑州黄河游览区
Yellow River Tourist Zone, Zhengzhou
12 郑州二七纪念塔
Monument Pagoda to February 7 Workers'
Uprising, Zhengzhou

10

12

11

河南

13、14 关林 位于洛阳市南郊 8 公里处，又
称关帝庙，是纪念三国时期蜀将关羽的墓葬之
地。初建于唐代，现存建筑多建于明、清。关
冢封土高达 12 米，据说关羽的头颅埋葬于此。
庙内的石狮、古碑、奇柏等也很有名。

Guanlin　Eight kilometers south of the city of
Luoyang, Guanlin, also called Emperor Guan's
Temple, is a memorial temple complex of Guan
Yu, a famous general of the State of Shu during
the Three Kingdoms (220-280), who was
honored as a god by Chinese emperors. First
constructed during the Tang Dynasty (618-
907), the present complex are most Ming or
Qing buildings. The grave mound is 12 meters
high, and it was said Guan Yu's head was
buried here. The stone-carvings of lions,
ancient tablets and oddly shaped cypresses
in the temple are also famous.

15 开封相国寺内景
An interior view of the Grand
Chancellor's Temple, Kaifeng

17 开封铁塔　位于开封市东北隅的铁塔公园内。铁塔建于北宋年间，平面呈八角形，13层，通高 55 米。整个塔身用 28 种不同造型的铁褐色琉璃砖砌成，因而俗称"铁塔"。塔身砖面上还雕刻有动物、佛像等塑像和花纹。

Iron Pagoda　In a park of the same name in northeast of Kaifeng City, the Iron Pagoda was first built in the Northern Song Dynasty. The structure is made of iron-colors glazed bricks, patterned in 28 different styles, but from a distance the pagoda looks like it was made from iron. The 13 story octagonal pagoda is more than 55 meters high. On the brick basement are exquisite carved patterns of animals, Buddhist motifs and flora.

18

19

20

18 石窟寺　位于巩义市东北伊洛河北岸大力山下。石窟雕刻始于北魏宣武帝景明年间（公元500—504年）。现存石窟5处，佛龛250余座，大小佛像7700多尊。

Buddhist Cave Temples　The temples are at the foot of Mt. Dali on the northern bank of the Yiluo River in Gongyi City. Construction of the caves began during the Jingming reign period (500-504) of the Northern Wei Dynasty, and additions were made during the later dynasties. There are now 5 grottoes, more than 250 shrines and 7,700 Buddhist figures.

19 宋陵　位于巩义市西南。北宋九帝除徽、钦二帝被金囚掳，死于漠北以外，其余七帝均葬于此。陵区内还有后妃墓20余座，并葬有宗室及王公大臣，如寇准、包拯等，共计百余人。

Song Tombs　The Song Tombs are scattered over an area southwest to Gongyi. Seven of the nine emperors of the Northern Song Dynasty (960-1127) were buried here; the other two were captured and taken away by the Jin armies who overthrew the Northern Song in the 12th century. There were over 20 tombs for empresses and imperial concubines in the area. And royal members and ministers of the dynasty, such as Kou Zhun and Bao Zheng (both were famous ministers), were also buried in the area.

20 焦作神农山
　　Shennong Mountain, Jiaozuo

湖北省
HUBEI PROVINCE

湖北省地处长江中游、洞庭湖以北。春秋战国时为楚国地，汉时属荆州，唐、宋年间设鄂州（因此简称鄂），清置湖北省。全省面积 18 万多平方公里，人口 6000 多万，有汉、土家、苗、回、侗、满、蒙古等民族。省会武汉市。

湖北省地势西高东低。鄂西大巴山东段神农架为华中最高峰，海拔 3105 米。东南部为江汉平原，多湖泊，有"千湖之省"的称谓。

湖北省历史悠久，文化发达，是古人类活动的主要地区和中华民族的发祥地之一。在数十万年前，这里就有人类生息。战国时属楚国，产生了发达的楚文化。三国时是魏、蜀、吴争夺的焦点，赤壁之战等许多著名的战役都发生在这里。著名的旅游胜地有东湖、黄鹤楼、归元寺、古隆中、武当山、神农架、西陵峡、屈原祠、明显陵等，其中，武当山古建筑群和明显陵被联合国教科文组织列入《世界遗产名录》。

Hubei, a province in the middle reaches of the Yangtze River and to north of Dongting Lake, is abbreviated as *E*. During the Spring and Autumn and Warring States periods, it was the territory of the State of Chu. Under the jurisdiction of Jingzhou Prefecture in the Han Dynasty and Ezhou Prefecture in the Song Dynasty, it became a province during the Qing Dynasty. The 180,000-square-kilometer province is home to Hans, Tujias, Miaos, Huis, Dongs, Manchurians and other ethnic peoples, with a total population of 60 million. Wuhan is the provincial capital.

The province slopes from the west to the east. Shennongjia, eastern part of the Daba Mountain, sits in the west of the province, and its highest peak is 3, 105 meters above sea level. The Jianghan Plain, in the southeast of Hubei, has so many lakes that gain it a nickname of "Province of A Thousand Lakes".

Hubei, a land of long history and developed culture, was one of birthplaces of Chinese Nation. Primitive Society people lived there hundreds of thousand years ago, and advanced Chu Culture was also created here. During the Three Kingdoms Period, it became a major battlefield, and major battles include the famous Battle of Chibi. Hubei is endowed with a list of tourist attractions, such as the East Lake, Yellow Crane Tower, Guiyuan Temple, Longzhong Relics, Wudang Mountains, Shennongjia, Xiling Gorge and Memorial Temple of Qu Yuan. Ancient complex in the Wudang Mountains and Ming Xianling Tomb have been listed as the world cultural heritage sites by the UNESCO.

1 武当山紫霄宫
Zixiao Palace on Wudang Mountains

2-4 武当山风景名胜区　位于丹江口市，背依神农架林区。风景区面积约240平方公里，有72峰、36岩、24涧、9泉等胜景，主峰天柱峰海拔1612米。武当山不仅风光秀丽，也是中国道教名山和武当拳术的发源地。山上有历代文物古迹和明代所建的道教建筑群，规模宏大，庄严绮丽。1994年，武当山古建筑群被联合国教科文组织列入《世界遗产名录》。风景区内主要景观有金殿、紫霄宫、元和观、南岩等。

Wudang Mountains　Located southwest of Danjiangkou City, Wudang Mountains back onto the Shennongjia Forest. The major peak, Tianzhu (Heavenly Pillar), stands 1,612 meters high. Within an area of 240 square kilometers, there are 72 peaks, 36 rocks, 24 streams and 9 springs. With the amazing and marvelous natural scenery, it is a famous Taoist mountain and the birthplace of Wudang Martial Arts. Atop on the mountain are cultural and historical sites of different dynasties, as well as the majestic and solemn Taoist architectural complex built in the Ming Dynasty (1368-1644), which was inscribed on the World Heritage List in 1994. Major tourist spots include Golden Hall, Zixiao Palace, Yuanhe Taoist Monastery and South Roak.

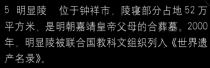

5　明显陵　位于钟祥市，陵寝部分占地52万平方米，是明朝嘉靖皇帝父母的合葬墓。2000年，明显陵被联合国教科文组织列入《世界遗产名录》。

Ming Xianling Tomb　Located in Zhongxiang City and covering an area of 52 hectares, it is the mausoleum of Emperor Jiajing's parents of the Ming Dynasty. It was inscribed on the World Heritage List by the UNESCO in 2000.

6 西陵峡
Xiling Gorge
7 屈原祠
Memorial Temple of Qu Yuan
8 洪湖风光
A view of Honghu Lake

9 荆州古城　位于长江中游北岸，是江汉平原上著名的历史文化名城。从东晋到五代，先后有五位帝王在此建都。原为土城，清代重建时改为砖城。这里扼守长江，形势险要，自古为兵家必争之地。"关羽大意失荆州"即发生在此。

Ancient City of Jingzhou　Situated on the northern bank of the middle reaches of the Yangtze River, Jingzhou is a city of great historical and cultural interest on the Jianghan Plain. It had been chose as the nation's capital by five Emperors from the Eastern Jin Dynasty (317-420) to the Five Dynasties (907-960). It was originally an earth city and rebuilt with bricks in the Qing Dynasty. The city holding access to the Yangtze River, had been a place contested by all strategists since ancient times. The famous historical event, "General Guan Yu lost Jingzhou negligently", happened right here.

10 黄鹤楼　位于武汉市武昌区蛇山之上。始建于三国东吴黄武二年（公元223年），曾为文人墨客聚集赋诗之处。历史上屡毁屡建。现存建筑为1985年仿清代式样重修。楼分五层，高51米，红柱黄瓦，层层飞檐，辉煌瑰丽，气势恢宏。

Yellow Crane Tower　Located on the Snake Hill in Wuchang District, Wuhan City, the tower was first built in 223 AD during the Three Kingdoms Period (220-280). After completion, the tower served as a gathering place for celebrities and poets to party and compose poems. It was destroyed and rebuilt many times in history. The present building was constructed in 1985 according to the style of architecture in the Qing Dynasty. The tower, 51 meters high, is five-storied with yellow tiles and red pillars, overlapping ridges and interlocking eaves, and looks magnificent.

湖南省
HUNAN PROVINCE

湖南省位于长江中游南岸，因地处中国第二大淡水湖——洞庭湖以南，而得名；又因境内第一大河湘江纵贯南北，故简称湘。全省面积21万多平方公里，人口6400多万，有汉、苗、土家、侗、瑶、回、维吾尔、壮、白等民族。省会长沙市。

湖南省自然资源丰富，有"鱼米之乡"、"有色金属之乡"、"非有色金属之乡"和"旅游胜地"的美称。该省历史悠久，景色优美，文物古迹众多，有省级以上风景名胜区25处，自然保护区22处。主要旅游景点有世界自然遗产武陵源、南岳衡山、岳麓山、洞庭湖、岳阳楼、马王堆汉墓、桃花源等。

湖南省人杰地灵，人物辈出，相传轩辕氏、祝融氏、舜帝都曾在此留下遗迹；开国领袖毛泽东的故乡也在这里。名人胜迹主要有韶山毛泽东故居、花明楼刘少奇故居、汨罗屈子（屈原）祠、耒阳蔡侯（蔡伦）祠、炎帝陵等。

Hunan is situated in the south of the middle reaches of the Yangtze River. Its name, meaning "south of lake", was derived from the fact that the province is located south of Dongting Lake, the second largest freshwater lake in China. Because of Xiangjiang River, which flows across the province from south to north, Hunan is also called "*Xiang*" in short. Covering a total of 210,000 square kilometers, the province has a population of 64 million consisting of Hans, Miaos, Tujias, Dongs, Yaos, Huis, Uygurs, Zhuangs, Bais and other ethnic peoples. Changsha is the capital.

Hunan abounds in natural resources, and is reputed as "land of fish and rice", "land of nonferrous metal", "land of ferrous metal" and "ideal destination for travelling". The province has a long history, and its landscape is magnificent. There are 25 national and provincial scenic resorts, 22 nature reserves at or above the provincial level, and large numbers of places of cultural interest within its territory. Major attractions of Hunan are Wulingyuan Scenic Resort, a world natural heritage site, Hengshan Mountain, the South Sacred Mountain of China, Yuelu Mountain, Dongting Lake, Yueyang Tower, Han Tombs of Mawangdui and Taohuayuan Tourist Zone.

Hunan is home to numerous men of great renown. It was said that Xuanyuan, Zhurong, Emperors Shundi and Yandi once lived there and left remains. Hunan is also the home province of Mao Zedong, the founder of the People's Republic of China, and numerous other outstanding historical figures. Memorial sites for figures of great renown include Mao Zedong's former home in Shaoshan, Liu Shaoqi's former home in Huaminglou, Qu Yuan's Memorial Temple in Miluo, Cai Lun's Memorial Temple in Leiyang and Tomb of Emperor Yandi.

武陵源风景名胜区
Wulingyuan Scenic Area

2-5 武陵源风景名胜区　位于湖南省西北部，面积264平方公里，峰峦如林，造形奇特，景观丰富，以奇峰、怪石、幽谷、秀水、溶洞"五绝"闻名于世。武陵源有山峰近3000多座，中心景区包括张家界国家森林公园、索溪峪、天子山等，是天然的动、植物园和地质公园。1992年，被联合国教科文组织列入《世界遗产名录》。

Wulingyuan Scenic Area　Covering an area of 264 square kilometers, the Wulingyuan Scenic Area is located in the northwest of Hunan Province, with almost 3,000 peaks standing in various characters. It is famous for marvelous peaks, grotesque rocks, tranquil valleys, beautiful water and magical karst caves. The scenic area includes Zhangjiajie National Forest Park, Suoxi Valley and Tianzi Mountain. It is a natural zoo, botanical garden and geological park. It became a UNESCO's world heritage site in 1992.

6、7 衡山 坐落于湖南省中部，是著名的五岳之一的"南岳"和道教五大名山之一。山势雄伟，南至衡阳，北到长江，盘行400余公里。共有72峰，主峰祝融峰，海拔1290米。衡山历史悠久，殿宇、古刹、碑刻等文物古迹众多，主要有祝融殿、藏经殿、南岳大庙、方广寺、南台寺、魔镜台等。祝融峰之高，藏经殿之秀，方广寺之深，水帘洞之奇被誉为"衡山四绝"。

Mt. Hengshan   Located in the center of Hunan Province, Mt. Hengshan is one of the Five Sacred Mountains and one of the Five Most Famous Mountains of Taoism. Its 72 peaks form a range serpentining for as far as 400 kilometers from Hengyang in the south to the Yantze River in the north. The summit, Zhurong Peak, rises 1,290 meters high. The Southern Sacred Mountain has a long history, which has bestowed it abundance of cultural relics as halls, monasteries and steles. Main tourist spots include Zhurong Hall, Hall of Storing Sutras, Nanyue (Southern Sacred Mountain) Temple, Fangguang Temple, Nantai Temple, Magic Mirror Terrace and so on. The tallness of Zhurong Peak, gracefulness of Hall of Storing Sutras, seclusion of Fangguang Temple and wonder of Water Curtain Cave are reputed as four marvelous spectacles of the mountain.

6

7

8 通道回龙桥
Circling Dragon Bridge, Tongdao Dong
Nationality Autonomous Prefecture
9 永顺县猛洞河
Mengdong River, Yongshun County

10．11 凤凰古城　位于湘西土家族苗族自治州南部、沱江之畔。古城山川秀丽，历史悠久，已有1300多年建城历史。这里至今较完整地保留了明清时期形成的传统格局和历史风貌。

Fenghuang (Phoenix) Ancient Town　The town is situated on the western boundary of Hunan Province and in the south of Xiangxi Tujia and Miao Nationalities Autonomous Prefecture. In an area of outstanding natural beauty where mountains, water and blue skies prevail, this ancient town with a history spanning 1300 years has a number of remarkable old buildings, whose architectural designs date from the Ming and Qing Dynasties.

12、13　岳麓山□东临湘江，西屏长沙，海拔300多米，自古即以山幽景美闻名。山上有爱晚亭、清风峡、蟒蛇洞、岳麓书院等景观。其中，岳麓书院坐落于山之东麓，始建于宋开宝九年（公元976年），是宋朝四大书院之一。清光绪二十九年（公元1903年），变为高等学府。1925年，改为湖南大学。

Yuelu Mountain　Situated in the west bank of Xiangjiang River, the Yuelu Mountain with an altitude of more than 300 meters, has been famous for secluded environment and beautiful scenery since ancient time. Tourist spots on the mountain are Pavilion of Loving to Evening, Gorge of Refreshing Breeze, Python Cave and Yuelu Academy. The Yuelu Academy, located on the east slopes of the mountain, was first built in 976, or the ninth year of Song Emperor Kaibao's reign, being one of the Four Most Famous Academies of the Song Dynasty. It was transferred to Institute of Higher Learning in 1903, and became the Hunan University in 1926.

广东省
GUANGDONG PROVINCE

广东省简称粤，地处中国东南沿海，与香港、澳门临近。全省总面积18万平方公里，地势北高南低，丘陵广布，约占全省面积三分之二。沿海有珠江三角洲和潮汕平原。全省人口8600多万，有汉、瑶、壮、回、满、畲、苗等42个民族。广东是中国华侨最多的省份，潮汕、梅州和广州附近是全国著名的侨乡。省会广州市。

广东省历史渊源久远，早在10万年前就有"曲江马坝人"在此生活。近现代史的许多重大历史事件，如鸦片战争、辛亥革命、北伐战争、广州起义均发生于此。

秀丽的山川，独特的景观，以及悠久璀璨的岭南文化，共同造就了广东省丰富的旅游资源。主要名胜古迹有：西樵山、鼎湖山、丹霞山等国家重点风景名胜区、越秀公园、华南植物园、星湖、陈家祠、南越王墓、中山故居等景点，此外还有锦绣中华园、中国民俗文化村、世界之窗等新景观。

Guangdong Province in south China, with an abbreviation of "Yue", sprawls on the shore of the South China Sea and is in close proximity to the Hong Kong and Macao special administrative regions. Covering an area of 180,000 square kilometers, the province has a topography that slants downwards from north to south. Two thirds of the region is hilly land, and the Pearl River Delta and Chaoshan Plain make up the rest. The population of the province is 86 million. The inhabitants include the people of Han, and 41 minority ethnic groups of Yao, Zhuang, Hui, Manchu, She, and others. Guangdong has the largest population of returned overseas Chinese, with Chaozhou, Shanzhou, Meizhou and Guangzhou areas as their major homes. Guangzhou city is the provincial capital.

Guangdong has a quite long history.

As early as more than 100,000 years ago, Qujiang Maba Man, the middle Paleolithic primitive man, once lived in present Guangdong's territory. Many significant events in Chinese modern history happened here.

Magnificent landscape, unique scenes and long and splendid Lingnan Culture — these wealth of tourist resources have given rise to a comprehensive tourist industry in Guangdong. Xiqiao, Dinghu and Danxia mountains are national key scenic resorts. Other scenic spots and sites of historial interest include Yuexiu Park, Botanical Garden of South China, Ancestral Temple of Chen Family, Memorial Hall of Dr Sun Yat-sen. Additionally, "Splendid China", a garden of miniature Chinese landscapes, China Folk Culture Village and the Park of Window of the World are newly developed tourist attractions.

1 广州华南植物园
Botanical Gardenof South China, Guangzhou

2 广州华南植物园
Botanical Garden of South China,
Guangzhou

3 广州五羊雕像
Sculpture of the Five Rams, Guangzhou

4、5 越秀公园 位于广州市中心，占地84万平方米，由3个人工湖和7座山岗组成。主要景观有镇海楼、五羊雕像等。其中，镇海楼高28米，分五层，登楼可揽广州市全貌。广州也被称为〝羊城〞，五羊雕像为其标志。

Yuexiu Park   Yuexiu Park in downtown Guangzhou has an area of 84 hectares, consisting of three artificial lakes and seven hillocks. Main scenic spots include Zhenhai Tower and the Sculpture of the Five Rams. Zhenhai Tower is a 28-meter-high Ming building, with five storeys and commanding a bird's-eye view of the whole city. The Sculpture of the Five Rams is the symbol of Guangzhou. According to an ancient and beautiful legend, Guangzhou is also called "City of Rams", or "Goat City".

6—9 陈家祠 位于广州市中山七路,是清末广东72县陈姓的合族宗祠和书院,也是广东现存规模最大、保存最完好、装饰最精美的古代艺术建筑群。陈家祠始建于清光绪十六年（公元1890年）,建筑面积1.3万平方米。祠内建筑以装饰精巧、富丽堂皇著称,荟萃了岭南木雕、砖雕、陶雕、灰雕、铜铁铸造、壁画、年画等建筑装饰,具有重要的历史、艺术、文化和科学价值。

Ancestral Temple of the Chen Family　Sitting on the seventh Zhongshan Road in Guangzhou, it was first built in 1890 or the 16th year of Qing Emperor Guangxu's reign, with donations of members of the Chen family who lived in the 72 counties of Guangdong Province. Covering a total area of 1.3 hectares, it is the largest, best preserved and best decorated ancient cluster of architectures in Guangdong. The temple is especially renowned for its beautiful decorations, including wood carving, brick carving, pottery carving, stone carving, lime carving, brass and cast iron, grotto, new year painting, and so on. These artistic decorations are important cultural relics of which possessing great value of history, art, culture and science.

10 广州中山纪念堂
   Sun Yat-sen Memorial Hall, Guangzhou
11 珠海渔女像
   Statue of Fishing-Girl, Zhuhai
12、13 珠海风光
   Scenery of Zhuhai

14、15 七星岩风景区 位于肇庆市北郊，面积7.6平方公里，主要景观为七岩、八洞、五湖、六岗，景点多达80个。七星岩因七座翠绿的山岩矗立湖滨，排列如北斗七星，而得名。风景区湖面广阔，风光秀丽，享有"桂林之山，西湖之水"的美誉。

Seven-Star Rocks Scenic Area　Lying in the northern suburbs of Zhaoqing, the area consists of seven rocks, eight caves, five lakes and six hillocks, having a total area of 7.6 square kilometers and more than 80 scenic spots. The seven razor-sharp monoliths covered with lush vegetation stand by a lake, like the Big Dipper in the firmament, hence the name. The picturesque landscape wins it the reputation of "Owning both the limestone peaks in Guilin and the water of West Lake in Hangzhou".

16 深圳
A view of Shenzhen
17 深圳世界之窗
Park of Window of the World,
Shenzhen

18 深圳香蜜湖
   Xiangmi Lake, Shenzhen
19 广州番禺虎门炮台
   Humen Battery in Panyu, Guangzhou

20 广州莲花山望海观音
Statue of Avalokitesvara of Overlooking
the Sea on the Lotus Mountain,
Guangzhou
21 中山市中山故居
Sun Yat-sen's former residence,
Zhongshan

22 佛山祖庙 始建于北宋元丰年间，明、清
两代多次重修、扩建。因其历岁久远，且为诸
庙首，故又称"祖庙"。祖庙占地面积约3500平
方米，庙内建筑和装饰，如陶塑、砖雕、石雕、
灰塑等都是不可多得的艺术珍品。

Ancestral Temple in Foshan   The original
temple was first built during the Northern Song
Dynasty, and has been developed through
renovations and additions in the Ming and Qing
dynasties. Therefore, it is called the Ancestral
Temples owing to its long history. The temple
covers an area of 3,500 square meters. Its
buildings and beautiful decorations such as
pottery, brick, and stone carvings are important
cultural and art relics.

21

22

23

24

23 西樵山　位于南海市的西南部。西樵山群峰拥翠，泉、瀑、岩、洞错落其间，风光绮丽景致优美，有"绿色翡翠"之美称。景区总面积29平方公里，景点众多，以白云洞最为著名。

Xiqiao Mountain　With its clear springs, grotesque rocks, fantastic crags and bizarre caves, Xiqiao Mountain in Nanhai, 29 square kilometers in area, has long been reputed as "the Green Emerald". There are many attractions in the mountain area but the surroundings of Baiyun Cave in the western part capture the essence of all beautiful scenery.

24 昭关金鸡石
Golden-Cock Rock, Shaoguan

广西壮族自治区

广西壮族自治区简称桂，地处中国南疆，南临北部湾，西南与越南交界。全区面积 23 万多平方公里，人口 4489 万，主要有壮、汉、瑶、苗、侗、仡佬、毛南、回、京、水等民族。自治区首府南宁市。

广西壮族自治区地形略成盆地状，岩溶地貌发育完全，石灰岩分布约占全区面积的一半；因高温多雨，溶蚀成千姿百态的峰林、岩洞，山水独特，风光绮丽，尤以桂林为最。广西的国家重点风景名胜区有桂林漓江、桂平西山、左江花山风景区等，还有八角寨、大桂山等 11 个国家森林公园以及北海银滩，柳州鱼峰山、柳公祠、兴安灵渠等旅游景点。此外，在广西居住的壮、瑶、苗、侗等少数民族的民俗风情，各具特色，异彩纷呈。

With Southeast Asia in close proximity to the south and sitting adjacent to Viet Nam, the Guangxi Zhuang Autonomous Region on the northern extremity of the Beibu Bay is abbreviated as *Gui*. It spreads over an area of 230,000 square kilometers and has a population of 44.89 million consisting of Zhuangs, Hans, Yaos, Miaos, Dongs, Gelaos, Maonans, Huis, Gins, Suis and other ethnic peoples. The capital city is Nanning.

The terrain of Guangxi is shaped like a basin. As typical of a karst landform, limestone formations cover almost half of the land. High temperatures and abundant rainfall have corroded the limestone into a forest of ridges, and peaks and caves with different shapes and characteristics, which gives rise to spectacular natural wonders that won Guangxi a lot of adages, such as "Guilin's landscape is unmatched under heaven". There are 3 national scenic reserves — Lijiang River, Xishan and Huashan, and 11 national forest parks, including Bajiaozhai, Daguishan, and so on. Other tourist attractions are Beihai's Silver Beach, Yufeng Mountain, Lord Liu's Temple, and Lingqu Canal. The Zhuangs, Yaos, Miaos, Dongs and many other ethnic minority people in Guangxi are known for their time-honoured and distinct folklores.

1 桂林山水
The landscape of Guilin

桂林市　桂林位于广西东北部，市区面积500多平方公里，是著名的风景旅游城市和历史文化名城，也是中国优秀旅游城市。典型的喀斯特（岩溶）地貌构成了"山青、水秀、洞奇、石美"的桂林山水奇景。著名的风景区有漓江、象鼻山、叠彩山、伏波山、芦笛岩、七星岩等。

Guilin　Situated in the northeastern part of Guangxi, Guilin proper covers an area of over 500 square kilometers. The world-renowned scenic city is one of the national famous historical and cultural city and excellent tourist city in China. A distinctive karst landmass is the reason behind Guilin's fabulous landscape that is characterized by green mountains, sparkling waters, strange caves and statuesque monoliths. Famous scenic areas in Guilin are Lijiang River, Elephant-Trunk Hill, Folded Brocade Hill, Whirlpool Hill, Reed Flute Cave and Seven-Star Cave.

2-5 桂林山水
The landscape of Guilin
6 三江程阳风雨桥
Chengyang Wind and Rain Bridge, Sanjiang
Dong Autonomous Prefecture
7 北海银滩
Silver Beach, Beihai

8 乡村景色
  A view of countryside of Guangxi
9 容县真武阁
  Zhenwu Pavilion, Rongxian County
10 德天瀑布　　位于中越边境大新县，是世界第二大的跨国瀑布。瀑布宽200多米，三级跌落，声闻数里，气势磅礴，蔚为壮观。

Detian Great Waterfall　　Located in Daxin county of Nanning City in Guangxi, Detian Waterfall along the Sino-Vietnamese border is the second largest transnational waterfall in the world. The grand three-tier waterfall is about 200 meters wide during the flood season, making a deafening sound, which could be heard several kilometers away.

海南省
HAINAN PROVINCE

海南省简称琼，位于中国最南端，北隔琼州海峡与广东省相望，包括海南岛和西沙群岛、南沙群岛、中沙群岛的岛礁及其领海。1988年4月，海南建省，省会海口市。海南省面积3.4万平方公里，人口787万，主要有汉、黎、苗、回等民族。

海南岛是中国第二大岛，中部为五指山，海平原、台地占全省面积的三分之二，森林覆盖率超过50%，属于热带季风气候，是中国热带作物基地。

海南岛风光秀丽，气候宜人，是中国著名的热带风光旅游胜地，以阳光、沙滩、海水和温泉著称。主要旅游城市有海口、三亚；名胜古迹有海瑞墓、五公祠、东郊椰林、天涯海角、大东海、亚龙湾、鹿回头、南湾猴岛，以及黎、苗族村寨等。

Abbreviated as *Qiong*, Hainan Province is located at the southernmost tip of China, facing Guangdong Province across the Qiongzhou Strait. Covering an area of 34,000 square kilometers, the province consist of Hainan Island, Xisha, Nansha and Zhongsha islands on the South China Sea, and their surrounding territorial waters. Established as a province in April 1988, Hainan has a population of 7.87 million at present including ethnic groups of Hans, Lis, Miaos, Huis and others. Haikou is the provincial capital.

The Wuzhi (Five-Finger) Mountains sits in the center of Hainan Island, the second largest island of China, and coastal plains and tablelands make up two-thirds of total area of the province. A half provincial territory covered by forest, Hainan is under a tropical marine monsoon climate, and is a base of tropical crops and plants in China.

Having fabulous scenery and pleasant climate, Hainan is nice tropical destination of scenic tour in China, and famous for sunshine, beaches, sea water and hot spring. Haikou and Sanya are major tourist cities of the province. Hainan woos visitors from around the world with a myriad scenic spots and places of cultural interest. These include Hai Rui's Tomb, Five Lords' Temple, Dongjiao Coconut Plantation, Tianya Haijiao, Dadonghai Beach, Yalong Bay, Luhuitou and villages of Li and Miao ethnic groups.

1 槟榔林
Areca Trees

2 椰岛风情
A view of the "Coconut Island"

3 海瑞墓 位于海口市秀英区。海瑞（公元1515—1587年），生于琼山，是明代著名的政治家，有"海青天"之誉。海瑞墓建于明万历十七年（公元1589年），墓高3米，圆顶，墓前立有4米高的石碑。

Tomb of Hai Rui   Hai Rui (1515-1587) was a compassionate officer and noted stateman of the Ming Dynasty. He was famous for his righteousness and royalty, and reputed as "Hai qingtian" (an upright magistrate is often likened to qingtian). The Tomb of Hai Rui, built in 1589 during Ming Emperor Wanli's reign, is located in Xiuying District, Haikou City. The tomb, 3 meters in height, is a semi globe shape brick structure. A stone tablet with Hairui's title inscripted on it was erect in front of the tomb.

4 黎村 海南省约有120万人口为少数民族。其中，黎族是海南岛最早的居民，至今保留着许多独特的民族风俗和生活习惯，"三月三"为其最著名的民俗活动。

Village of Li Ethnic Minority   Among the total population of 7.87 million of Hainan, 1.2 million people are minority ethnic groups. Lis are the earlier inhabitants of the island, and they keep many unique folklore and customs. The Third Day of the Third Lunar Month Festival is the most famous traditional festival.

5 万泉河 发源于五指山，全长163公里，是海南主要河流之一。两岸风光旖旎，别具南国风韵。

Wanquan River   The 163-kilometer-long Wanquan River, which originates in Wuzhi Mountains, is one of Hainan Province's main rivers. Beautiful scenery on both banks boasts the river a unique charm of southern China.

6

6 天涯海角　位于三亚市西南26公里处。这里海天一色，沙滩银白，立有上百块大小不一的奇石，中央一块高约10米的巨石上刻有"天涯"二字，为清雍正十一年（公元1733年）崖州太守程哲手迹，后清末文人刻有"海角"二字，还有南天一柱、海判南天等巨石雄峙。

Tianya Haijiao   26 kilometers southwest from Sanya, Tianya Haijiao (literally edge of the sky, rim of the sea) is a somber-looking beach with clear water, silver sands and a hundred-odd grotesque rocks in various shapes. Standing in the center is a huge rock, about 10 meters in height, inscribed with Chinese characters of "Tianya", the handwriting of Cheng Zhe, an officer of Yazhou, in 1733, or the 11th year of Qing Emperor Yongzheng's reign, and the characters of "Haijiao", added by literaty of the ends of the Qing Dynasty. Other attractions, such as Nantian Yizhu and Haipan Nantian, are also well known.

7 亚龙湾　位于三亚市东南28公里处，总面积18.6平方公里。亚龙湾三面青山相拥，一面呈月牙形向大海敞开，沙滩平缓宽阔，沙粒洁白细软，海水清澈澄莹，被誉为"天下第一湾"。

Yalong (Asian Dragon) Bay   The crescent-shape bay, 28 kilometer southeast of Sanya City, is screened by green hills in three sides, with a total of 18.6 square kilometers. It is reputed as "the Number One Bay Under Heaven" for the gentle and broad beach, white and soft sands, and crystal clear seawater.

7

重庆市简称渝，位于中国西南地区中部，长江和嘉陵江汇合处。1997年成为中国第四个直辖市。全市面积8.23万平方公里，人口3000多万，有汉、回、苗、土家等民族。

重庆地处四川盆地东部，北、东、南三面环山，素有"山城"之称。长江由西南向东北斜贯而过，穿山越岭，浩荡东流，形成著名的长江三峡。该市属中亚热带季风气候，夏季闷热，为长江三大"火炉"之一；冬、春多浓雾，年平均雾日100至150天，被称为"雾都"。

重庆市历史悠久，是中国历史文化名城之一。春秋战国时为巴国地域，隋唐时属渝州。元末明初为大夏国的国都。1927年设市。抗日战争时期为国民党政府陪都。重庆著名景点有世界文化遗产大足石刻，长江三峡，南、北温泉公园，红岩村革命纪念馆，白公馆，枇杷山等。

Abrreviated as "*Yu*", Chongqing is located in the center of northwestern China where the Yangtze River and Jialing River meet. It became the fourth municipality directly under the Central Government in 1997. With an area of more than 82,300 square kilometers, Chongqing has a total population of 30 million, including Hans, Huis, Miaos, Tujias and other ethnic peoples.

Situated in the eastern part of Sichuan Basin, Chongqing is screened by mountains in three sides of north, east and south, hence the nickname, "the Mountain City". The Yangtze River cross the province from southwest to northeast, and cuts through mountains. Here the river course suddenly narrows and the waters become turbulent. Sheer cliffs and steep mountains rise on either side, creating one of nature's most fantastic sights — the Three Gorges. Situated in the subtropical zone with a monsoon climate, Chongqing is hot and suffocating in summer, and is called one of the three "heating stoves" on the Yangtze River. Chongqing is also known as a "Fog City" due to the fact that it is wet and foggy in winter and spring, and it has 100 to 150 foggy days averagely in a year.

Chongqing enjoys a time-honored history. It is one of the famous Chinese cities endowed with historical and cultural significance. During the Spring and Autumn and the Warring State periods, it belonged to the State of Ba; it was in the territory of Yuzhou in the Sui and Tang dynasties, and became the capital of the State of Daxia during the late Yuan Dynasty. In 1927, Chongqing is incorporated as a city. During the War of Resistance against Japan, it was the "provisional capital" of China under the Kuomintang's rule. Major attractions include Dazu Rock Carvings, one of the UNESCO's world heritage sites, Yangtze River's Three Gorges, South and North Hot Spring Parks, Revolutionary Memorial Hall of the Red Crag Village, Bai's Mansion and *Pipa* (Loquat) Mountain.

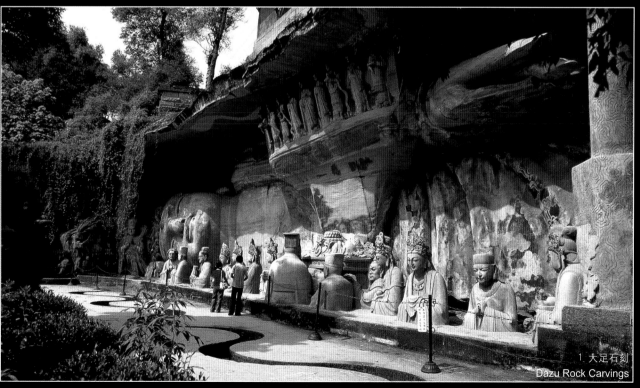

1. 大足石刻
Dazu Rock Carvings

2 大足石刻　位于重庆市"石刻之乡"大足县境内，这里保留有自唐宋以来的石刻造像70余处，雕像5万余尊，规模宏大，雕刻精美，题材多样，保存完整，以宝顶山、北山石窟摩崖造像最为集中，此外，还有南山、石篆山、石门山等处造像。石窟造像创建于晚唐，历经五代，完成于两宋，延续开凿250余年；以佛教造像为主，儒、道教造像并陈，是中国石窟艺术后期的杰出代表作品，也是世界石窟艺术的典范之一。1999年，联合国教科文组织将其列入《世界遗产名录》。

Dazu Rock Carvings　Dazu Rock Carvings in the county of the same name is best known for the stone carvings mostly on the Baoding-shan and Beishan mountains. There are more than 50,000 sculptures scattered over 70 points here. The large-scaled and best-preserved grottoes were constructed originally in the late Tang Dynasty and finished in the Song Dynasty, which lasted for more than 250 years. The sculptures, done in fastidious chisel work and gracious imagery are mostly images of Buddhism, and additionally, that of Confucianism and Taoism. Dazu Rock Carvings are outstanding representative of China's grottoes-building art at its later stages, as well as fine examples of grottoes art of the world. In 1999, it was inscribed on the World Heritage List by the UNESCO.

3　夔门
Kuimen
4　瞿塘峡
Qutang Gorge

5 张飞庙
  Zhangfei's Temple
6 石宝寨
  Shibao Village
7 白帝城
  Baidi City
8 丰都鬼门关
  "Gate of the Hell", Fengdu

9 朝天门码头
Chaotianmen Dock
10、11 重庆夜景
Chongqing at night
12 解放碑
Memorial to the Liberation
13 人民大礼堂
People's Assembly Hall

重庆市

四川省
SICHUAN PROVINCE

四川省位于中国西南地区、长江上游，简称川或蜀。全省面积48万平方公里，人口8329万，有汉、彝、藏、回、羌等民族，省会成都市。

四川省东部为海拔500米的四川盆地，西部为高原山脉，海拔3000米至4000米，地域广阔，气候复杂多样，农业发达，被誉为"天府之国"。

四川省旅游资源得天独厚，自然风光旖旎，名胜古迹甚多，有国家级风景名胜区9处，国家历史文化名城7座。其境内的青城山、都江堰、乐山大佛、峨眉山、九寨沟风景区、黄龙风景区均被联合国教科文组织列入《世界遗产名录》。四川省主要风景名胜有杜甫草堂、武侯祠、文殊院、望江楼、盐业博物馆、稻城风景区、蜀南竹海、海螺沟等。

Located in southwest China on the upper reaches of the Yangtze River, Sichuan Province, abbreviated as *Chuan* or *Shu*, has an area of 48 square kilometers and a population of 83.29 million composed of Hans, Yis, Tibetans, Huis, Qiangs and other ethnic peoples. Chengdu is the provincial capital.

The eastern part of the province is the Sichuan Basin with an altitude of 500 meters, and the west plateau is at an elevation from 3,000 meters to 4,000 meters above sea level. Having a vast territory and multiplex climate, Sichuan's agriculture is flourishing and reputed as "the Natural Storehouse".

Sichuan is endowed with rich resources of tourism. The province is known for its breathtaking natural beauty and many historical and cultural sites. There are 9 national scenic resorts and 7 national famous historical and cultural cities in Sichuan. Dujiangyan Irrigation Project, Mount Qingcheng, Giant Buddha of Leshan, Mount Emei, Jiuzhaigou Valley and Huanglong scenic areas have been inscribed on the World Heritage List by the UNESCO. Other key tourist spots are Du Fu's Thatched Cottage, Marquis of Wu's Temple, Wenshuyuan Monas-tery, Tower of Looking over the River, Salt Museam, Daocheng Scenic Area, Jianmen Pass, Bamboo Sea in south Sichuan, and Conch Gully.

1 九寨沟风景区
Jiuzhaigou Valley Scenic Area

都江堰和青城山 都江堰，位于都江堰市西、岷江上游，是中国古代劳动人民创建的一项著名的巨大水利工程。工程始建于战国时期（公元前475年—公元前221年），由秦国蜀郡守李冰负责督建，两千年来一直发挥着巨大的防洪和灌溉作用。青城山，位于都江堰市西南，是中国道教的发祥地之一。山上有36峰、8大洞、72小洞、108景，以及11座道观。都江堰和青城山于2000年，被联合国教科文组织列入《世界遗产名录》。

Dujiangyan Irrigation Project and Mount Qingcheng Dujiangyan Irrigation Project, the long-established water conservation works, is located at Dujiangyan City lying in the upper reaches of Minjiang River, which is the longest tributary of Yangtze River. During the Warring States Period (475 BC - 221 BC), Li Bing, a governor of Shu in the Qin State, directed the construction of Dujiangyan Weir. For more than two thousand years the whole system has functioned perfectly, serving as not only as flood prevention but also as an immense source for irrigation as well as a means to facilitate shipping and wood drifting. Mount Qingcheng, southwest to Dujiangyan City, is one of the birthplaces of Taoism. It boasts 36 peaks, 8 big caves, 72 lesser caves and 108 scenic spots, as well as 11 Taoism monasteries and temples. In 2000, Dujiangyan Irrigation System and Mount Qingcheng were both inscribed on the World Heritage List by the UNESCO.

2 都江堰
　Dujiangyan Irrigation Project
3 李冰像
　Statue of Li Bing
4 青城山
　Mount Qingcheng

5 乐山大佛　位于四川省乐山市岷江东岸、凌云山麓，是中国最大的一尊石刻坐佛。大佛通高70□米，开凿于唐开元初年（公元713年），历时□年方才完成。1996年，乐山大佛被联合国教科文组织列入《世界遗产名录》。

Leshan Giant Buddha　The Giant Buddha sits on the eastern bank of the Minjiang River and on the western slope of Lingyun Hill. With the height of 70.7 meters, it is one of the largest stone sculptures of Buddha in the world. The construction of the statue began in 713, during the first year of the Emperor Xuanzong's reign period of the Tang Dynasty (618-907), and completed in the 19th year of Emperor Dezong (803), a total of 90 years. Taking the shape of a Maitreya, the gigantic stone sculpture faces Mount Emei, with the rivers flowing below his feet. In 1996, it became a world cultural heritage site by the UNESCO.

6-8 黄龙风景名胜区　位于阿坝藏族羌族自治州松潘县境内，由黄龙景区和牟尼沟景区两部分组成。其雄奇的山岳、险峻的峡谷、绚丽的草原风光、浩瀚的林海、众多的湖泊以及丰富的动植物资源和独特的民族风情，展示出一幅幅神奇瑰丽的画卷。1992年，黄龙风景名胜区被联合国教科文组织列入《世界遗产名录》。

Huanglong Scenic Area　Situated in Songpan County of the Aba Tibetan and Qiang Nationalities Autonomous Prefecture in Sichuan Province, the Huanglong Scenic Area consists of two parts: Huanglong and Mouni Gully. The area possesses various huge and exotic landscapes, such as the magnificent mountains, precipitous valleys, splendid grassland scenery, vast sea of forest, plenty of lakes, rich animal-plant resources, and unique folk customs, and these marvelous scenes are quite spectaculars. In 1992, the Huanglong Scenic Area became one of world natural heritage sites of the UNESCO.

9、10 九寨沟风景名胜区 位于阿坝藏族羌族自治州的九寨沟风景名胜区，自然风光优美，集翠海、叠瀑、森林、雪川、藏族文化风情于一体，有"人间仙境"的美誉。九寨沟的水自然天成，清洁纯净，色彩丰富，闻名中外。九寨沟植物种类十分丰富，还生活着大熊猫、金丝猴、天鹅等珍稀动物。1992年，联合国教科文组织将其列入《世界遗产名录》。

Jiuzhaigou Valley Scenic Area Locating in Songpan County of the Aba Tibetan and Qiang Nationalities Autonomous Prefecture, Jiuzhaigou Valley is reputed as a "Fairyland". An integration of green lakes, multi-layered waterfalls, forests and snow-mountains with Tibetan culture and customs, it becomes a well-known scenic area. The water of Jiuzhaigou Valley is widely known for its crystal clearness, pure transparency and rich colors. There are rich forest resources here, and many kinds of rare animals such as giant panda, snub-nosed monkey, and swan are living here. In 1992, UNESCO inscribed it on the World Heritage List.

11

11-13 峨眉山风景区　峨眉山坐落在四川盆地南部，距成都150公里，是中国佛教四大名山之一，传为普贤菩萨的道场。风景区面积300平方公里，主峰万佛顶，海拔3099米。风景区内群峰叠翠，自然风光秀丽，动植物资源丰富，被誉为"植物王国"、"动物乐园"，有"峨眉天下秀"之称。日出、云海、"佛光"、"圣灯"为峨眉山四大奇观。主要景点有万佛顶、报国寺、万年寺、伏虎寺等。1996年，联合国教科文组织将其列入《世界遗产名录》。

Mount Emei Scenic Area　Mount Emei lies in the southern area of Sichuan basin, 150 kilometers away from Chengdu. It is one of the four Sacred Buddhist Mountains in China, known as the place of Buddhist Rites of Puxian (Samantabhadra Bodhisattva). The whole mountain covers an area of 300 square kilometers. Wanfoding (Summit of Ten-Thousand Buddha), the main peak of Mount Emei, is 3,099 meters in elevation. It is rich in natural and cultural resource and carries several monikers: "Kingdom of Plants", "Paradise of Animals", and is particularly famous for the title, "Elegance of Mount Emei Under the Heaven". The four wonders of Mount Emei are the Golden Summit Sunrise, Sea of Clouds, Buddha's Halo and the Holy Lamp. The main attractions include Wanfoding, Baoguo Temple, Fuhu Temple, Wannian Temple and many other spots. In 1996, the UNESCO inscribed it on the List of World Heritage.

14 万年寺内景
An interior view of Wannian (Ten Thousand Years) Temple

12

13

14

15

15 杜甫草堂 位于成都西郊浣花溪畔，是唐代伟大现实主义诗人杜甫的故居。杜甫（公元712—770年），河南巩义市人，为躲避安史之乱，于唐乾元二年（公元759年）始，在此居住近4年，创作了千古名篇《茅屋为秋风所破歌》等240余首诗篇。

Du Fu's Thatched Cottage   Located on the side of the Flower-Washing Brook in the western suburbs of Chengdu, it is the former residence of the celebrated Tang Dynasty poet, Du Fu. Du Fu (712-770), born in Gongyi City, Henan Province, fled to Chengdu where he built a humble cottage and stayed for about four years. During these years, he composed more than 240 poems reflecting upon the misery of people, including one of his masterpieces, "the Song of Autumn Winds Destroying My Cottage". In this poem, he expresses his anxiety for the plight of other poverty-stricken scholars and the desire for shelter for all the poor. Most of the present buildings were constructed in the Qing dynasties.

16

17

18

19

16 眉山三苏祠
Sansu Temple, Meishan
17 福宝镇古民居
Ancient residences in Fubao Town
18 成都望江楼
Tower of Looking over the River, Chengdu
19、20 海螺沟
Conch Gully
21 四姑娘山
Mountain of the Four Girls

20

21

22 稻城风景区
Daocheng Scenic Area
23 贡嘎雪山
Gongga Mountain
24 甘孜塔公草原风景区
Tagong Grassland Scenic Area, Garze
25 泸定县泸定桥
Luding Bridge, Luding County
26 米亚罗风景区
Miyaluo Scenic Area

四川

27

28

27-29 蜀南竹海　位于宜宾市长宁县和江安县交界处，是中国惟一一处以竹林景观为主体的国家级重点风景名胜区。120平方公里的区域内分布有28座山峦，山上遍布楠竹，还有花竹、棉竹、湘妃竹等30多个品种。景区内竹林成片，茂密苍翠；泉水清冽，飞瀑高悬；空气清新，郁香沁人。竹海深处还有天皇寺、罗汉洞、天上宫、观云亭等众多景点。

Bamboo Sea in South of Sichuan　The Bamboo Sea sprawls on the border of Changning and Jiang'an counties in Yibin. It is the only major scenic area in the country proclaimed by the State Council stressed on bamboo scenery. 28 peaks scatter over the 120-square-kilometer area. The entire area is, as its name suggests, a vast stretch of bamboo groves. There are above 30 kinds of bamboos such as Nan Bamboo, Flower Bamboo, Cotton Bamboo, Imperial-Concubine-Xiang Bamboo and so on. The air is fresh, while streams run with a rich susurrus, and waterfalls tumble and splash — all these qualify the Bamboo Sea as an ideal bio-tourist destination. In a boundless expanse of green waves there are a lot of scenic spots, such as Heavenly Emperor Temple, Arhat Cave, Heaven Palace, Pavilion of Viewing Cloud, and so on.

29

贵州省
GUIZHOU PROVINCE

贵州省地处云贵高原东北部，简称黔或贵。全省面积17万余平方公里，人口3500多万，主要有汉、苗、布依、侗、彝、水、回、仡佬、壮、瑶等民族，是中国多民族的省份之一。省会贵阳市。

贵州省是一座巨大的天然公园，全省的山石、水景、洞穴等自然资源极其丰富。省内有黄果树瀑布、织金洞、红枫湖、舞阳河、龙宫等8个国家重点风景名胜区；遵义、征远等6座国家历史文化名城；以及青龙洞、增冲鼓楼等国家重点文物保护单位6处。此外，贵州是中国民族节日最多的地区。据统计，每年少数民族节日有1000多个，并且，节庆活动的地域性很强，即便是同一民族，由于住地不同，活动内容和节目的名称、时间也不尽相同。

Guizhou Province lies in the northeast part of the Yungui Plateau, abbreviated as *Qian* or *Gui*. It covers 170,000 square kilometers and has a population of 35 million. The polyethnic province is home to compact communities of varying ethnic backgrounds such as Han, Miao, Buyei, Dong, Yi, Sui, Hui, Gelao, Zhuang and Yao. Guiyang is the provincial capital.

Guizhou is a large natural park with rich resources of rocks, water bodies and caves. There are 8 national scenic resorts, such as the Huangguoshu Waterfall, Zhijin Cave, Red Maple Lake, Wuyang River, Dragon Palace, and so on. There are 6 national famous historical and cultural cities including Zunyi, Zhengyuan and others, and 6 sites under state protection as key cultural relics, such as Blue Dragon Cave and Drum-Tower in Zengcong. In addition, Guizhou holds the greatest number of China's ethnic festivals. Statistics show that more than 1,000 minority ethnic festivals are celebrated in this province every year. These festivals have a strong local flavour. As the dwelling places differ, even the same ethnic groups hold festivals with different names and activities, and on different dates. A distinct landscape, unique ethnic customs and habits, and a pleasant weather have turned Guizhou into an ideal tourist and holiday-making destination.

1　黄果树瀑布
Huangguoshu Waterfall

2

3

2 黄果树瀑布　位于安顺市，是中国最著名的瀑布景观。夏季水量充足时，瀑布宽约81米，落差70米，从崖顶泻落，倾入犀牛潭中，轰然巨响，气势磅礴，如万马奔腾。

Huangguoshu Waterfall　Huangguoshu Waterfall, the most famous waterfall in China, is about 70 meters long and 81 meters wide during the flood season. Its water rushes down to a pond named Xiniutan (Rhinoceros Pond) with thunderous roars, which can be heard a few kilometers away, like ten thousand horses galloping and shaking the ground and the hill. The scene of Huangguoshu Waterfall changes while you are standing in different places.

3 贵阳甲秀楼
　Jiaxiu Tower (First Scholar's Tower), Guiyang
4、5 贵阳黔灵山
　Qianling Mountain, Guiyang
6 贵阳花溪公园
　Huaxi (Flower Stream) Park, Guiyang

4

5

7 侗寨鼓楼
  Drum-tower in Dong Village
8 梵净山自然保护区
  Mt. Fanjing National Nature Reserve
9 赤水竹海
  Bamboo Sea in Chishui
10 安顺龙宫风景区
   Dragon Palace Scenic Area, Anshun

11 安顺红枫湖
Red Maple Lake, Anshun
12 赤水桫椤林
Groves of Cyathea Spinulosa in Chishui
13 遵义会议会址
The Site of Zunyi Meeting
14 镇远古城
Ancient Town of Zhenyuan
15 镇远青龙洞
Blue Dragon Cave, Zhenyuan

云南省

YUNNAN PROVINCE

云南省位于中国西南边陲，简称滇或云，面积38万多平方公里。战国时为滇国地，唐、宋时分属南诏和大理国，元代设置省。云南省人口4288万，是中国民族最多的省份，有汉、彝、白、哈尼、壮、傣、苗、回、拉祜等26个民族的人民生活在这里；其中，少数民族人口约占全省的三分之一、全国的七分之一。省会昆明市。

云南省地处云贵高原，山地约占全省面积94%，气候复杂多样，有上千种鸟兽和上万种植物，被誉为"动植物王国"。该省地理条件优越，自然资源丰富，文物古迹众多。丽江古城和"三江并流"被列入《世界遗产名录》；昆明、大理、丽江为中国历史文化名城；滇池、路南石林、西双版纳、玉龙雪山等均为国家重点风景名胜区；还有圆通寺、大观楼、翠湖公园、黑龙潭、世博园、曼飞龙塔、大理三塔、蝴蝶泉、苍山、洱海、泸沽湖等旅游景观。民俗节庆有路南火把节、橄榄坝泼水节、大理三月街等。

Also called *Dian* or *Yun* for short, the southwest Chinese province of Yunnan covers an area of over 380,000 square kilometers. During the Warring States Period (475BC-221BC), the region belonged to the State of Dian. In the Tang and Song dynasties, it was under the jurisdiction of the State of Nanzhao and Dali. During the Yuan Dynasty (1271-1368), Yunnan Province was installed. The province has a population of 42.88 million, it is the home to compact communities of 26 ethic peoples including Yi, Bai, Hani, Zhuang, Dai, Miao, Hui, Lahu, and others. The population of minority nationalities makes up one third of the province's total population or one seventh of the China's, making Yunnan a province with most ethnic minority in China. Kunming is the provincial capital.

Yunnan is situated on the Yungui Plateau, and mountains account for 94 per cent of the province's total area. Its complicated and varied climates make it a best home to thousands of birds, animals and plants, which win it a reputation of "the Kingdom of Plants and Animals." Yunnan is rich in resources of tourism for its favorable conditions of geography, rich resources of nature and countless cultural relics and historical sites. Old Town of Lijiang and the Three Parallel Rivers are world heritage sites, and Kunming, Dali and Lijiang are all national famous historical and cultural cities. Dianchi Lake, Stone Forest of Lunan, Xishuang Banna, and Jade Dragon Snow Mountain are listed as National Important Scenic Resorts. Other attractions are Yuantong Temple, Grand View Pavilion, Emerald Lake Park, Black Dragon Pool, Site of the World Horticultural Exposition of Kunming, Manfeilong Pagoda, Three Pagodas at Dali, Butterfly Spring, Cangshan Mountain, Erhai Lake, Lugu Lake, and so on. Among the original folk festivals held here are the Torch Festival in Lunan, Water-Splashing Festival in Olive Dam and the Third Month Street Fair of Dali.

1 丽江古城
Old Town of Lijiang

2-6 丽江古城　国家历史文化名城丽江，位于云南省西北部，总面积3.8平方公里，是一座以纳西族为主要居民的古老城镇。始建于宋末元初（12世纪末至13世纪中叶）。古城的民居融合了汉、白、纳西、藏等民族的文化，形成了独有的建筑风格。独具特色的东巴文化、纳西古乐、白沙壁画更是古城悠久丰富的历史文化的见证。1997年，丽江古城被联合国教科文组织列入《世界遗产名录》。

Old Town of Lijiang　As a state-level ancient cultural town, Lijiang is located in the northwest of Yunnan Province, and covers an area of 3.8 square kilometers. The town has a history of 800 years. At the end of the Southern Song Dynasty (1127-1279), the Naxi (also spelt Nakhi or Nahi) ethnic group moved here and built the town. The town is famous for its unique layout. Combining the architecture styles of Han, Tibetan, Bai and other ethnic groups, the old town still preserves in its overall structure, the traditional natural aesthetics of the Naxi people and their interest in life. And the Dongba Culture, Naxi Ancient Music and Baisha Frescos are the testimonies of the long and rich traditional culture of the town. It was inscribed on the List of World Heritage by the UNESCO in 1997.

7

7 昆明滇池
Dianchi Lake, Kunming
8 昆明大观楼
Grand View Pavilion, Kunming
9 昆明世博园
Site of the World Horticultural
Exposition of Kunming
10 昆明黑龙潭公园
Black-Dragon-Pool Park, Kunming

8

9

10

三江并流自然景观 位于云南省西北部地区。"三江并流"是指源自青藏高原唐古拉山的金沙江、澜沧江和怒江三条大河流入横断山脉纵谷地带，并行奔流 400 公里的壮观景象。整个区域面积4万余平方公里，由八大片区组成，是世界上生物物种最丰富的地区之一。2003 年，三江并流自然景观被列入《世界遗产名录》。

Three Parallel Rivers of Yunnan Protected Areas   Consisting of eight geographical clusters of protected areas within the boundaries of the Three Parallel Rivers National Park, in the mountainous northwest of Yunnan province, the 40,000-square-kilometer region features sections of the upper reaches of three great rivers of Asia: the Yangtze, Mekong and Salween — namely, the Jinsha, Lancang and Nu rivers — run roughly parallel about 400 kilometers, north to south, through steep gorges of the Hengduan Mountains. The site is an epicentre of Chinese biodiversity. It is also one of the richest temperate regions of the world, in terms of biodiversity. In 2003, UNESCO inscribed the Three Parallel Rivers of Yunnan Protected Areas on the World Heritage List.

11 三江并流景区：梅里雪山
    Meili Snow Mountain of the Protected
    Areas of Three Parallel Rivers
12 三江并流景区：虎跳峡
    Tiger-Jumping Gorge of the Protected
    Areas of Three Parallel Rivers
13 三江并流景区：白茫雪山
    Baimang Snow Mountain of the Protected
    Areas of Three Parallel Rivers

14

14-16 玉龙雪山 位于丽江北15公里处，是长江南岸第一高山，由13座山峰组成，最高峰海拔5596米，常年积雪，由北向南绵延35公里，犹如一条凌空飞舞的玉龙，因此得名。

Yulong Snow Mountain   Yulong (Jade-Dragon) Snow Mountain, located 15 kilometers north of Lijiang, is the highest mountain on the sourthern bank of the Yangtze River. It has a total of 13 peaks extending 35 kilometers from south to north, like a huge flying jade dragon, hence the name. The main peak with an altitude of 5,596 meters above sea level, is snow-capped nearly 365 days per year.

15

16

17-20 石林　位于石林彝族自治县，总面积达350平方公里，为典型的喀斯特岩溶地质奇观。整个风景区由大小石林、乃古石林、大叠水瀑布、月湖、芝云洞地下石林、奇风洞等7个景区组成。景区内千千万万个石峰、石柱，拔地而起，姿态各异，被誉为"天下第一奇观"。石林地区居住着彝族撒尼人。每年农历六月二十四日，是彝族传统的火把节，届时将在此举行隆重的节庆活动。

Stone Forest　Covering a total area of 350 square kilometers, the Stone Forest, a topographical turmoil wrought by a jungle of 100 or so groups of monoliths in shapes ranging from overhanging cliffs to grotesque boulders, is situated in the Shilin Autonomous County of the Yi Nationality. It consists of seven scenic areas — the Big and Small Stone Forests, Naigu Stone Forest, Dadieshui Waterfall, Moon Lake, Subterranean Stone Forest in Zhiyun Cave, and Cave of Magical Wind. Thousands of stone peaks and stone pillars, taking in various shapes such as pagodas, spears, animals or human being figures, are scattered here and there. It is reputed as "the most fantastic scenery under heaven". The natural spectacle is made all the more alluring by its inhabitants, the Sani people, whose peculiar habits and customs never fail to keep the visitors mesmerized. Grand celebrations are held during the Torch Festival, which falls on the 24th day of the 6th lunar month.

18

19

20

21

21 昆明圆通寺
Yuantong Temple, Kunming

22 昆明翠湖公园
Emerald Lake Park, Kunming

23 昆明红嘴鸥
Red-beak gulls

24 大理蝴蝶泉
Butterfly Spring, Dali

25 大理古城
Ancient Town of Dali

23

24

22

26 大理三塔 位于苍山山麓，因比立于原崇圣寺前，又称崇圣寺三塔。千寻塔最高，高69.13米，为正方形16层密檐式砖塔，结构形建属于典型的唐代风格。两座小塔均高约42米，10层八角形，建于五代年间，塔身雕有精美图案。1978年重修三塔时，发现大批唐宋时期珍贵文物。

Three Pagodas in Dali   The three Pagodas arise on the Mt. Cangshan slopes overlooking the Erhai Lake. They are also called the Three Pagodas of Saintly Worship for their location in front of the former monastery with the same name. Qianxun Pagoda, the tallest of the three, has 16 tiers and reaches a height of 69.13 meters. It is a close-eaved square brick pagoda built in an architectural typical style of the Tang Dynasty (618-907). The two smaller octagonal pogodas, each 42 meters high with 10 tiers, have a luxurious appearance with their exquisite carvings. They were built in the Five Dynasties (907-960). Many precious relics of the Tang and Song dynasties were discovered in the Three Pogodas during the 1978 reconstruction, which make them even more famous.

25

云南

Erhai　Just as its name implies, the Erhai (Ear Lake, literally), a fresh-water lake two kilometers northeast of Dali, is similar in form of that of an ear. Covering 250 square kilometers and an average altitude of 1,966 meters, the blue, rippling lake and the snow-covered Mt. Cangshan, located on the western shore, add radiance and beauty to each other. The scene is, therefore, described as "Silver Mt. Cangshan and Jade Erhai".

30

28 剑川石窟甘露观音
Statue of Manna-Avalokitesvara of
Jianchuan Grottoes
29 剑川石窟
Jianchuan Grottoes
30 香格里拉
A beautiful view of Shangri-la
31 香格里拉奶子河
Naizi River in Shangri-la

32、33 泸沽湖　位于宁蒗彝族自治县和四川
省盐源县交界处。湖面海拔 2685 米，总面积近
50 平方公里，水面似镜，景色优美。湖畔为纳
西族居住区，当地保留着传统的母系社会生活
方式。

Lugu Lake　The Lugu Lake is located on the
border of Ninglang Autonomous County of the
Yi Nationality, Yunnan Province and Yanyuan
County, Sichuan Province. The lake occupies
an area of almost 50 square kilometers, with
an altitude of 2,685 meters. The water is green
and clear, and the surrounding environment
is well preserved. The lake shore is inhabited
by Mosuo People, a branch of Naxi group, who
lives in log cabins and retains the vestiges of
a matriarchal society.

31

32

33

34 西双版纳橄榄坝
Olive Dam, Xishuangbanna

35 元阳梯田
Terraced fields, Yuanyang

36 瑞丽风光
A view of Ruili

37 元谋土林
Earth Forest, Yuanmou

38 曼飞龙塔 又叫笋塔，位于景洪市大劫龙
江乡，建于1204年，共有9座白塔坐落在八角
形须弥座之上，主塔居中，高16.29米，八座
副塔分建在八个角上，高近9米，塔身雕有佛
龛，结构精美，具有典型的傣族建筑风格。

Manfeilong Pagoda　Also called the Bamboo
Shoot Pagoda for its shape, the Manfeilong
Pagoda lies in Damenglong Village in Jinghong
City. It was built in 1204. The pagoda building
on an octagonal basement actually consists
of nine stupas, with the primary stupa in the
center while the eight small stupas clustering
to its base. The primary stupa rises 16.29
meters, and each small stupa has a height of
about 9 meters. Niches are carved in the body
of stupas. The Manfeilong Pagoda has a
typical Dai style of architecture.

西藏自治区
TIBET AUTONOMOUS REGION

西藏自治区简称藏，位于中国的西南边疆，总面积120多万平方公里，人口262万，有藏、汉、门巴、纳西、珞巴、回等民族。首府拉萨市。

西藏为"世界屋脊"青藏高原的重要组成部分，平均海拔在4000米以上。唐古拉山绵延其北，喜马拉雅山耸立其南，东有横断山，西有昆仑山，中部有念青唐古拉山和冈底斯山，共同构成了西藏独特的地理景观。在雪域高原众山之中，遍布江河湖泊。雅鲁藏布江是西藏最大的河流，被藏族视为"摇篮"和"母亲河"。西藏还有大小湖泊1500多个，总面积为2.4万多平方公里，约占中国湖泊总面积的三分之一。

悠久的历史和独特的宗教文化造就了西藏色彩缤纷的风俗民情以及众多的人文景观。西藏共有寺庙2700多座，其中布达拉宫、大昭寺、罗布林卡等均被联合国教科文组织列入《世界遗产名录》。主要旅游城市有拉萨、日喀则、江孜等。

Situated in southwest China, Tibet Autonomous Region is also called "*Zang*" for short. The region covers 1.2 million square kilometers, and has a population of 262 million, which includes Tibetan, Han, Monba, Naxi, Lhoba and Hui. The capital is Lhasa.

Being the main body of the Qinghai-Tibet Plateau, Tibet at an average elevation of over 4,000 meters is reputed as "the Roof of the World". Lofty mountains—Tanggula in the north, the Himalayas in the south, Hengduan in the east, Kunlun in the west, and Nyainqentanglha and Gangdise in the center—form the unique topography of Tibet with their astonishing heights. The land of snows is criss-crossed by rivers. The Yarlung Zangbo, the mightiest river of Tibet, cutting a foamy, ferocious 2,091 kilometers course eastward in the southern part of Tibetan Plateau, is regarded as "the Cradle of Tibet" or "the Mother River" by locals. Ensconced in tall mountains and scattered on the vast land are also 1,500 lakes with a total area of more than 24,000 square kilometers, or one third of the total area of lakes in China.

Besides the spectacular sceneries, the long history and unique religious culture have bestowed Tibet colourful folklore and customs, and numerous culture relics. Tibet possesses more than 2700 temples, among which the Potola Palace, Jokhong Monastery and the Norbulinka are UNESCO-endorsed world culture heritage sites. Main tourist cities are Lhasa, Xigaze and Gyangze, and so on.

1 布达拉宫
The Potala Palace

2、3 布达拉宫　坐落于拉萨红山上，是藏传佛教胜地之一。公元7世纪，松赞干布迎娶尼泊尔和大唐公主为妃，并在此山上建造皇宫，即布达拉宫营建的肇始。宫殿占地9万平方米，高约120米，共13层，主体建筑分为红宫和白宫。布达拉宫是藏族文化艺术的宝库，存放有经文、佛像、唐卡等大量珍贵文物。1994年，被联合国教科文组织列入《世界遗产名录》。

The Potala Palace　One of the famous tourist spots of Lamaism, the Potala Palace is situated on the Red Mountain in Lhasa. Later in the 7th century, upon marrying Princess Wencheng of the Tang Dynasty and the Nepalese princess, Songtsen Gampo decided to build a grand palace — the Potala — to accommodate them and to serve as a memorial to the important event. About 120 meters in height and 360 in width, and occupying a space of 90,000 square meters, the complex is divided into two sections: the Red and White palaces. It is the quintessence of ancient Tibetan architecture, and a treasury of Tibetan culture and arts. Many precious cultural relics such as sutras, images of Buddha, Thangkas, were kept in the palace. In 1994, UNESCO inscribed it on the List of World Heritage.

4、5 从大昭寺远眺布达拉宫
A distant view of the Potala from Jokhong Temple
6 金碧辉煌的布达拉宫
The splendid Potala

5

6

7 弥勒菩萨塑像
  Statue of Maitreya Bodhisattva
8 坛城
  The Mandala
9 唐卡
  Thangka

11

10、11 大昭寺　始建于647年，是西藏最早的木结构藏传佛教寺院，既体现唐代建筑风格，又具有西藏和尼泊尔的建筑风格。寺内藏有大量珍贵文物，最著名的是释迦牟尼12岁时等身镀金佛像。█000年，大昭寺被联合国教科文组织列入《世界遗产名录》。

Jokhang Monastery   Built in 647, the Jokhang Monastery is the earliest wood-masonry structure in Tibet. The temple is the product of Han, Tibetan and Nepalese architectural techniques. It is in possession of a collection of invaluable cultural relics. The most famous and valuable of these is the sculpture of Sakyamuni aged 12. It became a world heritage site of the UNESCO in 2000.

12

12、13 罗布林卡　藏语意为"宝贝花园"，是历代达赖喇嘛夏季办公场所，又称为"夏宫"。面积近40万平方米，始建于18世纪40年代，园内金碧辉煌，花木繁盛，为西藏最富特色的园林之一。2001年█罗布林卡被联合国教科文组织列入《世界遗产名录》。

Norbulingka   Meaning "the Treasure Park" in Tibetan, Norbulingka has a total of 40 hectares. First built in the 1740s , it used to be the palace where Dalai Lama ruled and received officials in summers, so it was also called the Summer Palace. Landscaped providently with pavilions, water-front chambers, lakes and winding footpaths, the palace looks more like a south Chinese garden. It was inscribed on the List of World Heritage by the UNESCO in 2001.

13

14

中国风景名胜

14-16 珠穆朗玛峰　位于定日县南、中国与尼泊尔交界处，藏语意为"女神第三"，为喜马拉雅山主峰。山峰海拔8848.13米，是世界最高峰，被誉为"世界第三极"。山顶终年冰雪覆盖，冰川长达26公里，极为壮观。周围环绕有38座山峰，海拔均在7000米以上。珠穆朗玛峰吸引着世界众多的登山爱好者。

Mt. Everest　Located in Tingri County, Mt. Everest, also known as Mt. Qomolangma, meaning the Third Goddess in Tibetan, is main peak of the Himalayas and the highest peak in the world. Standing 8,848.13 meters above sea level, the peak, snow-capped throughout the year, lies at the border between China and Nepal, and is reputed "the Third Pole of the world". Massive glaciers extending 26 kilometers, feature a thrilling splendor. The place is actually clustered with 38 peaks at heights of more than 7,000 meters. The peak has been a holy climbing attraction for world's mountaineers.

17 喜玛拉雅山
The Himalayas

19

18 然乌错
Lake Ra'og co
19 拉萨河
Lhasa River
20 神山圣湖
Holy Mountain and Lake

20

21、22 纳木错 位于当雄县境内，藏语意为
"天湖"，面积 1961 平方公里，湖面海拔 4718
米，是世界最高的咸水湖，为西藏"四大圣湖"
之一。海拔 7162 米的念青唐古拉山坐落在湖
畔。湖水清澈湛蓝，山峰白雪皑皑，相映成趣，
蔚然壮观。

Namco Lake   Namco, meaning the Heavenly
Lake in Tibetan, is located near Damxung
County. 4,718 meters above sea level and
covering a total of 1,961 square kilometers,
the lake is the highest saltwater lake in the
world, and respected as one of the Four Holy
Lakes in Tibet by Buddhist pilgrims. The snow
capped Mt. Nyainqentanglha, 7,162 meters in
altitude, soars up to sky beside the lake,
forming a delightful contrast. Singing streams
converge into the clean sapphire blue lake,
which looks like a huge mirror framed and
dotted with flowers.

21

22

23　错高湖
　　Lake Conggo
24　班公错鸟岛
　　Bird Isle on the Lake Pangkog
25　羊八井地热
　　Geothermal resources of Yangbajain

陕西省
SHAANXI PROVINCE

陕西省简称陕或秦，位于黄河中游。全省面积19万平方公里，人口3600多万，有汉、回、满、蒙古等民族。省会西安市。

该省历史悠久，周初即称陕西，春秋战国时为秦国地，唐属关内、山南等道，宋初置陕西路，元起设陕西行省。从公元前11世纪起，先后有13个王朝在此建都，共有73个帝王曾在这里统治。

陕西省的历史文化在中华文明史上占有重要地位。全省共有各类文物点3.5万多处，其中，古人类遗址60余处、古墓葬4300多处（大型帝王墓葬72座），庙观1200多座，石窟557处，还有古建筑、石刻、近现代建筑和史迹近2万处。秦始皇陵和兵马俑已被联合国教科文组织列入《世界遗产名录》。陕西的历史文化名城市有西安、咸阳、延安、榆林、韩城、汉中等。主要风景名胜有骊山、华山、天台山、大雁塔、小雁塔、昭陵、乾陵、黄帝陵、华清池等。

Shaanxi Province is a landlocked province in the middle reaches of the Yellow River, with the abbreviation of *Shaan* or *Qin*. Covering an area of more than 190,000 square kilometers, it has a population of 36 million of Hans, Huis, Manchurians, Mongolians and other ethnic peoples. The capital of the province is Xi'an City.

As early as the Zhou Dynasty, it was called the present name of Shaanxi.It belonged to the State of Qin in the Spring and Autumn and Warring States periods, Guannei and Shannan circuits in the Tang Dynasty, Shaanxi Circuit in the Song Dynasty. Shaanxi was established as a province in the Yuan Dynasty. 13 dynasties had their capital cities in the province, with a total of 73 emperors ruling supreme there.

The venerated culture of Shaanxi plays an important role in Chinese civilization history. The province is dotted with more than 35,000 cultural relic sites, including 60-odd palaeoanthropologic and Paleolithic and Neolithic sites, 4,300 ancient tombs, of which 72 are large-scale tombs of emperors, more than 1,200 temples and monasteries, 557 grottoes, and 20,000 or so other historical sites of stone carvings, ancient and modern buildings. Mausoleum of Emperor Qin Shihuang had become a world heritage site. Xi'an, Xianyang, Yan'an, Yulin, Hancheng and Hanzhong are national famous historical and cultural cities. Main tourist spots in Shaanxi are Lishan, Huashan, and Tiantai mountains, Big and Lesser Wild-Goose Pagodas, Zhaoling and Qianling tombs, Mausoleum of the Yellow Emperor, Huaqing Palace, and so on.

1 兵马俑
Terra-cotta Warriors

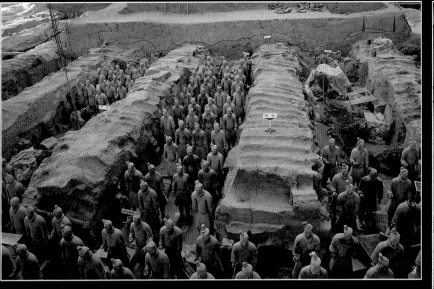

2-5 秦始皇陵及兵马俑　秦始皇陵位于骊山脚下，是统一中国的第一个皇帝——秦始皇嬴政的陵园。陵区占地56.25平方公里，按照当时都邑的模式建造。兵马俑坑位于陵园东侧1500米处，由三个呈品字形排列的俑坑组成，是秦始皇陵的陪葬坑。已发掘的7000余件陶俑、陶马，形象千姿百态，个性特征表现得惟妙惟肖，被誉为"世界第八大奇迹"。1987年，联合国教科文组织将秦始皇陵及兵马俑列入《世界遗产名录》。

Mausoleum of Emperor Qin Shihuang and Terra-cotta Warriors　The Mausoleum of Emperor Qin Shihuang, Yingzheng, who was the first emperor unified China, is located at the foot of Lishan Mountain, Shaanxi Province. Covering an area of 56.25 square kilometers, the mausoleum was designed according to the capital then. The vaults of the terra-cotta warriors and horses are 1.5 kilometers east of the mausoleum. There were totally over 7,000 pottery figures unearthed there, including soldiers, chariots and horses. It is known as "the Eighth Wonder in the World". In 1987, the United Nations Educational, Scientific and Cultural Organization (UNESCO) inscribed the Mausoleum of Emperor Qin Shihuang and Terra-cotta Warriors on the World Heritage List.

6 华清池　位于临潼县南骊山西北麓，距西安 30公里。此处因有适宜洗浴医疗的温泉，而成 为历代帝王建筑行宫别墅之所。华清宫建于唐 天宝六年（公元747年），曾为唐明皇和杨贵妃 避暑、游玩和沐浴的地方，素有"温泉水滑洗 凝脂"的美称。

Huaqing Palace　South of Lintong County and 30 kilometers to the east of Xi'an, the Huaqing Palace sits on the northwest slopes of Mount Lishan, where served as a popular site to build temporary palaces by emperors of different dynasties for its hot spring for convalescence. The Huaqing Palace was built in 747, or the sixth year of Tang Tianbao's reign. Emperor Minghuang of the dynasty and the Lady Yang, his favorite concubine, used to stay here for sightseeing and bathing.

7 大雁塔　坐落于西安市南大慈恩寺内，是中 国名塔之一。建于唐永徽三年（公元652年）， 为安置高僧玄奘由印度带回的佛经而建。塔立 于台基之上，通高64米，共7层，砖木结构， 气势雄伟。登塔眺望，可俯览西安古城风貌。

Big Wild Goose Pagoda　Located in the south of Xi'an, the famous pagoda stands in what was formerly the Temple of Great Maternal Grace. The original pagoda was built in 652 AD to house the Buddhist scriptures brought back from India by the traveling monk Xuan Zang. Standing on a terrace, the Big Wild Goose Pagoda is an impressive, seven-storey, wood and brick building with a totally height of 64 meters. It offers a full view of the ancient Xi'an City when one climbs to the top of the pagoda.

7

8

8-10 华山　古称西岳，是中国历史上五大名山之一，位于关中平原东部华阴市南。华山由五座山峰组成，山势险峻奇秀，素有"自古华山一条路"之誉，最高峰落雁峰海拔2200米。华山景区面积达300平方公里，景点众多，各具特色，被列为国家重点风景名胜区。

Mount Huashan　One of the Five Sacred Mountains in China, Mount Huashan is located on the eastern part of Guanzhong plain and south in Huayin City, and it was known as the Western Sacred Mountain in ancient times. Huashan, true to its reputation as the "most precipitous mountain under heaven", is a cluster of five peaks with Luoyan Peak, the highest peak of 2,200 meters above sea level. Covering a total area of 300 square kilometers, the scenic area is dotted with multitudinous tourist spots with their distinctive characteristics, and is a national scenic resort.

9

10

11

12

11 黄河乾坤弯
   Universal Bay of the Yellow River

12 黄帝陵 位于延安黄陵县北桥山。黄帝姓姬，号轩辕氏，生于寿丘（今山东省曲阜市），死后葬桥山，是中华各族人民的共同祖先。黄帝陵高3.6米，周长48米，墓前立有碑亭，内置"桥陵龙驭碑"。山麓还建有轩辕黄帝庙，庙内有汉武帝亲手种植的古柏。

Tomb of King Huangdi King Huangdi, whose first name was Ji and nickname was Xuanyuan, was born in Shouqiu (Qufu City in Shandong Province), and buried on the slopes of Mount Bridge in Huangling County, Yan'an City. He was believed the ancestor of Chinese. The tomb is 3.6 meters high, 48 meters in periphery, with a tablet pavilion in front of it, in which stands the tablet with inscription of "The Dragon's Burial Palace on Mount Bridge". At the foot of the mountain stands the Temple of King Huangdi, Xuanyuan by name, in which grows the cypress tree planted by Emperor Wudi of the Han Dynasty.

甘肃省
GANSU PROVINCE

甘肃省简称甘或陇，位于黄河上游，地跨青藏、内蒙古、黄土三大高原，海拔大都在1000米以上。全省面积39万平方公里，人口2562万，主要有汉、回、藏、蒙古、土、裕固、保安、东乡、哈萨克、撒拉等民族。省会兰州市。

甘肃省是中国旅游业较发达的地区之一，为探访古代文明的旅游胜地。驰名中外的"丝绸之路"，贯穿东西，留下了历朝各代修建的石窟、建筑等1000余处丰富多彩的文物名胜。踏上1600公里的汉唐丝绸之路，沿途有素称"世界艺术宝库"的敦煌莫高窟、长城嘉峪关、兰州五泉山、白塔山、天水麦积山石窟、永靖炳灵寺石窟、夏河拉卜楞寺、榆中兴隆山、张掖大佛等古迹。甘肃省有鸣沙山、麦积山、崆峒山3个国家重点风景名胜区，有敦煌、天水、武威、张掖4座国家历史文化名城，12处全国重点文物保护单位。敦煌莫高窟被联合国教科文组织列入《世界遗产名录》。

Abbreviated as *Gan* or *Long*, the northwest Chinese province of Gansu spans the Qinghai-Tibet, Inner Mongolia and Loess plateaus in the upper reaches of the Yellow River. It covers a territory of 390,000 square kilometers, with an average elevation of more than 1,000 meters above sea level. Gansu has a population of 25.62 million, which embraces the Hans, Huis, Tibetans, Mongolians, Tus, Yugurs, Bonans, Dongxiangs, Kazaks, Salars, and so on. The capital is Lanzhou City.

As one of advanced areas of tourism in China, Gansu is an ideal place to seek out the roots of the ancient civilizations of the world. There are more than 1,000 ancient sights attributed to different periods, including ancient grottoes, old buildings, and a rich variety of cultural relics discovered along the legendary Silk Road. The 1,600-kilometer-long Silk Road of the Han and Tang dynasties unfailingly brings the visitors to such places as Dunhuang Mogao Grottoes (known as a veritable world-class treasure house of art), Jiayu Pass on the Great Wall, Five-Spring Mountain and White Pagoda Mountain in Lanzhou, Maijishan Grottoes in Tianshui, Grottoes of the Bingling Temple of Yongjing, Labrang Temple of Xiahe, Xinglong Mountain of Yuzhong, Giant Buddha Monastery of Zhangye. There are 3 national scenic resorts — Echoing-Sand Mountain, Maijishan Mountain, Kongtong Mountain, 4 national famous historical and cultural cities — Dunhuang, Tianshui, Wuwei, Zhangye, and 12 key cultural sites under state protection in Gansu. Dunhuang Mogao Grottoes was a world cultural heritage site.

1 嘉峪关
Jiayu Pass on the Great Wall

2 敦煌莫高窟　俗称千佛洞，凿建于敦煌市东南25公里的鸣沙山东麓峭壁之上。洞窟始建于前秦建元二年（公元366年），后经历朝修建，工程近千年，规模宏大，是中国最著名的石窟之一。莫高窟南北长约1600多米，现存大小洞窟492个，壁画4.5万多平方米，彩塑2400余尊，是一座集建筑、绘画、雕塑、宗教以及民风民俗于一体的综合文化艺术宝库。1987年，联合国教科文组织将其列入《世界遗产名录》。

Dunhuang Mogao Grottoes　Also known as the Caves of A Thousand Buddhas, the Mogao Grottoes is set into the steep cliff of Echoing-Sand Mountain about 25 kilometers southeast of Dunhuang City. This honeycomb of caves was constructed almost a millennium, beginning in 366, or the second year of the Emperor Jianyuan's reign of the Pre-Qin Dynasty. With a length of 1600 meters from south to north, it is one of the most famous and largest grottoes in China. A total of 492 grottoes, 45,000 square meters of murals and 2,400 painted statues remain now. It is a treasury of arts including architecture, painting, sculpture, religion and folklore. In 1987, UNESCO inscribed it on the List of World Heritage.

3 敦煌莫高窟牌坊
Arch of the Dunhuang Mogao Grottoes
4、5 鸣沙山
Echoing-Sand Mountain
6 月泉阁
Pavilion of the Crescent Lake

7 月牙泉　位于鸣沙山北麓。泉水汇聚成湖，在沙丘环抱之中，犹如一弯新月，因此得名。该泉两千多年来从未枯竭，被誉为"沙漠第一泉"。

Crescent Lake　　Located on the north slopes of Echoing-Sand Mountain, the Crescent Lake was formed by spring water trickling up into a depression between huge sand dunes, forming a crescent-shaped pond, hence the name. The Crescent Lake has remained free from the encroachment of sand and never dried up, and was reputed as "the Number One Spring in the Desert".

9

8 嘉峪关 位于嘉峪关市西南，为明代长城西端终点，也是"丝绸之路"的必经之地，自古便为军事要塞，有"天下雄关"之称。关城建于明洪武五年（公元1372年），周长733米，面积3.35万平方米，高10余米，6米以下为黄土夯筑，以上用土坯加固。现为全国重点文物保护单位。

Jiayu Pass   Situated to the southwest of the city of the same name, Jiayu Pass is the western terminal of the Ming Great Wall. Sitting on the celebrated Silk Road, the pass was also reputed as "the Magnificent Pass Under Heaven" for its military position as a stronghold in ancient times. The pass was built in 1372 or the fifth year of the Hongwu Reign of the Ming Dynasty, with a circumference of 733 meters, a height of 10.7 meters and an area of 33,500 square meters. The pass's lower part of the wall, six meters in height, is built of rammed earth, and the upper part is solidified with adobe. It is one of the key cultural sites under state protection.

9 阳关
Yang Pass on the Great Wall
10 长城第一堆
First Mound of the Jiayu pass on
the Great Wall
11 雅丹地貌
Yadan Wind-Erosion Landform
12 汉长城遗址
Ruined site of the Han Dynasty Great Wall
13 野骆驼群
Wild camels

14 玉门关　位于敦煌市西北约90公里处，为
汉代西陆两关之一，是丝绸之路进入西域北道
和中道的必经关口。

Yumen Pass　One of the two Han-Dynasty
fortifications in the West Territory, the Yumen
Pass stands some 90 kilometers to the northwest of Dunhuang City, providing access from
Dunhuang to the West Territory by way of the
northern and middle sections of the Silk Road.

青海省
QINGHAI PROVINCE

青海省简称青，位于中国西北部，与甘肃、四川、西藏、新疆等省、自治区相邻。全省面积72万多平方公里，人口510万，主要有汉、藏、回、土、撒拉、蒙古、哈萨克等民族。省会西宁市。

青海，在古时属西戎地，汉为羌地，隋置西海、河源等郡，唐宋为吐蕃地。1928年，建青海省。

青海省地处"世界屋脊"——青藏高原东北部，平均海拔3000米以上，地势西高东低，遍布名山大川。主要山脉有：唐古拉山、阿尔金山、祁连山、昆仑山等。中国许多著名的河流，如长江、黄河、澜沧江等，均发源于该省。

壮丽的山河和悠久的历史造就了青海丰富的旅游资源。主要名胜古迹有塔尔寺、青海湖、西宁清真大寺等。

Qinghai Province, abbreviated as "*Qing*", is situated in northwestern China, and adjacent to Gansu, Sichuan, Tibet and Xinjiang. Covering an area of more than 72 million square kilometers, Qinghai has a population of 5.1 million, and it is home to compact communities of varying ethnic backgrounds such as Han, Tibetan, Mongol, Hui, Tu, Salar and Kazak. Xining is the capital of Qinghai.

In ancient times Qinghai was the territory of the Western Rong Tribe. It was not until the Western Han that the Qiang people took control. During the Tang and Song, Qinghai was part of territory of the Tubo Kingdom. In 1928, it was incorporated as a province.

Situated in the northeast part of Qinghai-Tibet Plateau, which known as the "Roof of the World", Qinghai has an average altitude of 3,000 meters above sea level. The province is high on the relief map in the west but low in the east. In its tettitory, there are many famous mountains — Tanggula, Aljin, Qilian and Kunlun. Many noted rivers, such as the Yangtze, Yellow and Lancang, rise here.

Its awesome mountains, mighty rivers and venerated history have bestowed an abundance of tourist resources on Qinghai. Main tourist attractions include Tar Monastery, Qinghai Lake, and Grand Mosque of Xining.

1 青海湖
Qinghai Lake

2 日月山 位于青海湖东南，属祁连山脉，海拔3489米。因土色呈红色，原名赤岭。传说唐文成公主入藏时经过此处，为表示进藏决心，将皇帝赐给的日月宝镜置于此，因此得名。山麓有流向独特的倒淌河景观。

Riyue Mountain   Located southeast to the Qinghai Lake, the Riyue (Sun and Moon) Mountain was formerly called Red Ridge because of its bald reddish rocky top. It stands at 3,489 meters in elevation and belongs to the Qilian Mountains. Legend has it the Princess Wencheng of the Tang Dynasty mounted the mountain on her way to Tibet, and put "the Precious Mirror of Sun and Moon", a gift from the Tang emperor, down the mountain to show her determination, hence the name. On the northwest side of the mountain, flows the Reverse River.

3 塔尔寺 位于湟中县鲁沙尔镇西南隅。该寺建于明嘉靖三十九年（公元1560年），是黄教创始人宗喀巴的诞生地，为中国藏传佛教格鲁派六大名寺之一。寺院占地40多万平方米，房屋达9000余间，依山势起伏而建，由大、小金瓦殿、大经堂等藏汉风格的建筑组成。

Tar Monastery   Built in 1560, the Tar Monastery is one of six major sanctuaries of the Gelug sect of Tibetan Buddhism, to be situated in Lusha'er, a town in Huangzhong County, because it was the birthplace of the sect's father, Tsong Kha-pa. The monastery covers an area of more than 40 hectares. Its 9,000 rooms, including the Greater and Lesser Golden-Tiled Temples, Grand Sutra Hall, are laid out on a well-conceived plan to perfectly hug the contours of a mountain, forming a phenomenal combination of Han and Tibetan architectures.

4-6 青海湖和鸟岛　青海湖位于青海省东北部，蒙古语称"库库诺尔"，意为青色的湖。湖面海拔3200米，面积4573平方公里，是中国最大的内陆咸水湖。位于青海湖西北部的鸟岛，被誉为"鸟的天堂"。鸟岛，面积0.8平方公里。每年5月，从东南亚、印度、巴基斯坦以及中国南方各地飞来的斑头雁、天鹅、棕头鸥、鸬鹚、秋沙鸭等多种候鸟，总数在10万只以上，在岛上栖息营巢，蔚为壮观。

Qinghai Lake and Bird Isle　Qinghai Lake in northeast Qinghai Province, 4,573 square kilometers in area and 3,200 meters in elevation, is the largest landlocked saltwater lake in China. The Mongolian call it "Koco Nur", which means blue lake. Bird Isle, a 0.8-square-kilometer peninsular in northwestern of the lake, is reputed as a "Bird Paradise". It is a habitat for more than 100,000 migratory birds, including bald-headed geese, geese, brown-headed gulls, cormorants, and ducks, arriving in May from Southeast Asia, India, Pakistan and South China. It is a magnificent sight that so many birds nest and dwell on the island.

5

宁夏回族自治区简称宁，位于中国西北部地区，黄河中上游，东邻陕西，北部和西部与内蒙古毗邻，南部与甘肃接壤。全区面积6.6万平方公里，人口562万，主要有回、汉、满等民族，其中，回族占三分之一。省会银川市。

宁夏，是一块美丽富饶的土地，地形以山地、高原为主，平原占全区1/4。自治区水利发达，土地富饶，物产丰富。古老的黄河流经该区397公里，滋润着千里沃野，被誉为"塞上江南"，又有"天下黄河富宁夏"之说。枸杞、甘草、贺兰石、发菜和羊皮被誉为宁夏红、黄、蓝、黑、白五色土特产。

由于历史悠久，地貌奇特，宁夏旅游资源十分丰富，银川为国家历史文化名城，主要景区、景点有西夏王陵、青铜峡、海宝塔、须弥山石窟、中卫高庙、沙坡头、南关清真寺、沙湖风景区等。

Ningxia Hui Autonomous Region, *Ning* for short, is located in the center of northwestern China and the middle and upper reaches of the Yellow River. Covering an area of 66,000 square kilometers, the region is bordered by Shaanxi, Inner Mongolia and Gansu. The ethnic Hui people make up one third of the local population of 5.62 million that also includes Han, Manchurian, and so on. Its capital is Yinchuan.

Most of the beautiful and richly endowed land is covered by mountains and plateaus, and the plain area makes up one fourth of the land. The Yellow River, 397-kilometers in Ningxia, has a drainage area of over 1,000 square kilometers. Crisscrossed by a labyrinth of waterways, and endowed with abundant natural resources, Ningxia is regarded as rich as the well-endowed area south of the Yangtze River. As the saying goes, " Of all the regions along the Yellow River, Ningxia is the most prosperous." Chinese wolfberries (red), licorice roots (yellow), Helan Stone (blue), hair weeds (black) and goatskins (white) are the five most famous native products of Ningxia.

Long history and unique landscape have bestowed an abundance of tourist resources on Ningxia. Yinchuan is one of national famous historical and cultural cities. Main tourist spots are Mausoleums of the Western Xia Kingdom, Qingtong Gorge, Haibao Pagoda, Sumeru Grottoes, High Temple, Shapotou, Nanguan Muslim Mosque, Sands Lake Scenic Spots, and so on.

1 沙漠风光
Scenery of desert

2 中卫高庙 位于中卫城北，始建于明永乐年间，称"新庙"。清康熙年间重修，改称"玉皇阁"。现存建筑多为清咸丰以后修葺重建。高庙，以高取胜，是宁夏古建筑中的杰作。在仅4000余平方米的高台上，筑有260多间重楼叠阁。该庙当年是儒、释、道三教合一的宗教场所，庙内共塑有各类神像174座。

High Temple at Zhongwei   Located north to Zhongwei County, the High Temple was first built in the period of the reign of Emperor Yongle (1368-1398) of the Ming Dynasty. The High Temple was originally called "the New Temple". By the Qing Dynasty, it became a large-scaled architecture complex. During the period of the reign of Emperor Kangxi of Qing Dynasty, it was renovated and renamed "Pavilion of Jade Emperor." The present complex were mostly constructed during and after Qing Emperor Xianfeng's reign. The temple is famous for its height. On a high terrace of about 4,000 square meters, buildings and pavilions involving more than 260 rooms were constructed. The High Temple is an outstanding representative of Ningxia's ancient architectures. It was a place for religious activities of Confucianism, Buddhism and Taoism. 174 statues of different religions are protected well in the temple.

3

4

3 沙坡头旅游区 位于中卫，北面是腾格里沙漠，南面是壮阔的黄河，中间是一片绿洲。中国四大鸣沙之一的"金沙鸣钟"，就在沙坡头的坡顶。这里不仅以丰硕的治沙成果饮誉世界，还因其独特的自然景观驰名中外，被誉为"世界沙都"。

Shapotou   Shapotou (Top of the Sand Slope) Tourist and Scenic Zone is located in Zhongwei County, bordered the Tengger Desert in north and the Yellow River in south. A number of oases lie right in the heart of the area. One of China's four humming sand dunes, "the Golden Sand and Humming Bell", is situated at the top of Shapotou. Nicknamed as "the Deserts Capital of the World", it is famous for not only its unique natural scenes, but also achievements of subduing the deserts.

4 西夏王陵 位于银川市西 30 公里的贺兰山东麓，是西夏（公元 1038 — 1227 年）历代帝王陵墓所在地。陵园面积 50 多平方公里，有 9座帝陵和 193 座王候勋戚的陪葬墓，规模宏大，造型奇特，被称为"中国的金字塔"。

Mausoleums of the Western Xia Kingdom   Nine kings of the ancient Kingdom of Western Xia (1038-1227) were buried in the area, 30 kilometers west to Yinchuan City on the eastern side of the Helan Mountain. In the 50-square-kilometer graveyard, there are also 193 tombs of high officials, generals and aristocrats of the kingdom. It is one of the largest and best-preserved imperial graveyards in China. The mausoleums are unique not only in structure but also in their sheer sizes and close proximity to each other, and are reputed as "the Pyramids of China".

5 银川南关清真寺
  Nanguan Muslim Mosque, Yinchuan

新疆维吾尔自治区
XINJIANG UYGUR AUTONOMOUS REGION

新疆维吾尔自治区位于中国西北边疆，简称新。全区面积160万平方公里，约占全国国土的六分之一，是中国面积最大的省份。自治区人口1900余万，有维吾尔、哈萨克、汉、回、柯尔克孜、蒙古等13个民族。自治区首府乌鲁木齐市。

新疆有三大山系：南为昆仑山、阿尔金山，北有阿尔泰山，中部横贯天山，将全区分割为南疆和北疆。南北各有一巨大盆地，分别为塔里木盆地和准噶尔盆地。境内还有中国最长的内陆河——塔里木河，最大的沙漠——塔克拉玛干沙漠和最低的盆地——吐鲁番盆地。

新疆自然景观奇特，历史文化悠久，旅游资源丰富，民族风情绚丽多彩。境内有国家重点文物保护单位14处，国家自然保护区3处，国家重点风景名胜区和国家历史文化名城各1处。主要景观有天山、天池、克孜尔千佛洞、高昌故城、楼兰古城遗址、天鹅湖、火焰山等。

The northwest Chinese border region of Xinjiang, abbreviated as "*Xin*", is the largest province in China with an area of more than 1.6 million square kilometers, or one sixth of Chinese total territory. Xinjiang's multiracial population of 19 million mainly consists of 13 ethnic peoples, including Uygurs, Kazaks, Hans, Huis, Kirgizsand and Mongols. The capital of the region is Urumqi.

Xinjiang has three main mountains: Kunlun-Aljin in south, Altay in north, and Tianshan in the center, which divides the region into north and south Xinjiang, each with a huge basin namely Junggar and Tarim. China's longest interior river, Tarim, the largest desert, Taklimakan, and the lowest basin, Turpan, are all in the region.

Peculiar natural scenery, long history, venerated culture, and splendid local folklore form Xinjiang's wealth of tourist resources. The region has fourteen key cultural sites under state protcetion, three national reserves, one national scenic resort and one national famous historical and cultural city. Main scenic spots include Tianshan Mountain, Tianchi Lake, Kizil Thousand-Buddha Grottoes, ruins of Gaochang Ancient City and Ancient Loulan, Swan Lake, Flaming Mountain, and so on.

↑ 天池
Tianchi Lake

2 天池 位于阜康市博格达峰西北山腰。湖面海拔1980米，面积4.9平方公里，池深90米。湖水清澈如镜，雪峰环抱，云杉挺拔，风景秀丽。

Tianchi Lake   Sprawling on the northwest side of Mt. Bogda like a sparkling pearl imbedded in Tianshan Mountain, the Tianchi Lake in Fukang City, is geologically a moraine lake 1,980 meters above sea level, 4.9 square kilometers in area and 90 meters deep fed by snow runoffs. Snow-mantled peaks and sky-piercing spruces, among other things, define Tianchi Lake as a scenic place with prismatic splendour.

3 草原风光
Scenery of grassland
4 天山
Tianshan Mountain
5 库尔勒天鹅湖
Swan Lake in Korla

6-8 赛里木湖　位于博乐市西南，海拔2073米，面积450平方公里，是新疆最大的高山湖泊。这里湖光山色，景致优美，坡地蒙古包点缀其间，湖岸是牛羊的天然牧场，每年的那达慕大会就在此举行。

Sayram Lake　　With an altitude of 2,073 meters above sea level, the 450-square-kilometer Sayram Lake to the southwest of Bole is Xinjiang's largest alpine lake. The grasslands and mountain slopes ashore are studded with yurts, while big herds of cattle and sheep graze in the meadows. During the Nadam Fastival, here is the site of a variety of merry-making activities.

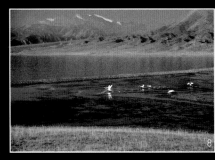

9 交河故城　位于吐鲁番西13公里雅乃尔孜河谷，是古代西域36国之一的车师前国的国都遗址。因地处两条河道的交汇之处，故名。现存遗址为唐代所建。故城建在30米高的土岸上，长1650米，宽约300米。故城内尚可辨认的建筑有塔、寺、民居等。

The Ruins of Jiaohe　Lying in Yarnaz Gully 13 kilometers west of Turpan, the ruins used to be the capital of Yarkhoto, one of 36 kingdoms of West Territory. The ancient city was first established during the Han Dynasty as a garrison town on a 30-meter-high loess plateau bounded by two rivers — thus the name Jiaohe, which means "confluence of two rivers". Present ruin of the city, built during the Tang Dynasty, is 1,650 meters long and 300 meters wide. Debris and dilapidated walls and bare foundations are what remain of the place, but the inexorable pace of history is nevertheless keenly felt from the city layout and vestiges of yamens, monasteries, pagodas and back alleys.

10　塔克拉玛干沙漠
The Desert of Taklimakan

11—14 哈纳斯湖
Kanas Lake
15 吐鲁番瓜果园
Orchards in Turpan

16–18 胡杨林
Huyang-tree forest
19 塔里木河
Tarim River

20

20 柏孜克里克千佛洞　位于吐鲁番市东北48公里处,火焰山西侧。千佛洞凿建于南北朝至元代,现存77个洞窟中,有40个保留有壁画,是研究新疆古代历史文化艺术的重要资料。

Beziklik Thousand-Buddha Grottoes Situated on the western side of the Flaming Mountains and 48 kilometers northeast of Turpan, the grottoes were Buddhist cave-temples built from the Northern and Southern Dynasties to the Yuan Dynasty. Remnants of murals are found in 40 of the 77 cave-temples that have remained to this day. The murals, colophons and text on them, furnish valuable material for the study on history, culture and art of Xinjiang.

21 魔鬼城
Ghost Town

21

22

22 火焰山　位于吐鲁番盆地偏北，东西长约100公里，南北宽约10公里，山为红砂岩构成，在强烈的阳光照射下，山体通红，犹如一条燃烧的火龙盘踞在吐鲁番盆地之中，故名。

Flaming Mountain　In the north of Turpan Basin lies the aptly-named Flaming Mountain, 100 kilometers long and 10 kilometers wide. Under the scorching sun, the mountain with red sandstone slopes looks like a flaming dragon coiled in the center of the Turpan Basin, and hence the name.

23、24 五彩湾
　　Five-Hued Bay

23

24

25 坎儿井　与万里长城和京杭大运河并称为"中国古代三大工程"。它主要分布在吐鲁番、哈密、木垒地区一带，是当地人民的一种特殊灌溉系统，主要功用是将雪山融水引往四面八方灌溉农田，具有结构简单、水源充足、不易蒸发等优势。仅吐鲁番的坎儿井总数就近千条，全长约5000公里，大多建于清朝时期。

The Karez System　An irrigation system of wells connected by underground channels, the Karez is considered as one of the Three Great Ancient Projects in China, the other two being the Great Wall and the Grand Canal. It is distributed mainly in Turpan, Hami and Mulei Area. The local people invented this ingenious irrigation technology by tapping abundant water underneath the arid Gobi Desert that surrounds the Turpan Basin. The water from melting snow and rain fall in the Karez would not evaporate in large quantities even under the scorching heat and fierce wind which ensuring a stable water flow and gravity irrigation. There are in the Turpan area nearly 1,000 Karez totaling 5,000 kilometers in length, which mostly built in the Qing Dynasty.

26 石头城
City of Stone

25

26

香港位于中国南部、珠江口东南，距广州市约140公里，由香港岛、九龙半岛、新界及周围岛屿组成。面积1000多平方公里，人口678万。居民中96％是中国人。使用中文和英文。

香港自古以来就是中国的领土。鸦片战争后被英国占领。1997年7月1日，中华人民共和国恢复对香港行使主权，设立特别行政区，并实行"一国两制"政策。

香港被誉为 "东方之珠"，不仅是国际主要金融、制造业、运输业及商业中心之一，而且自然景观秀丽迷人，旅游业发达，有"旅游购物天堂"之称。主要名胜有维多利亚公园、香港公园、太平山、海洋公园、宋城、香港会议展览中心、胡文虎花园等。

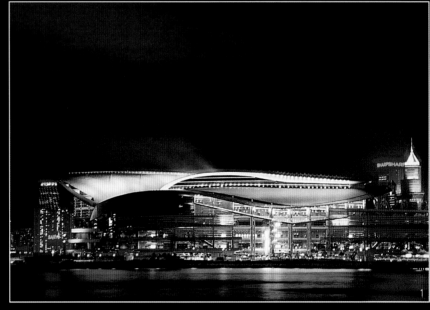

Located south to Guangdong Province and southeast to the mouth of the Pearl River, Hong Kong is about 140 kilometers from Guangzhou City. It is made up of Hong Kang Island, Jiulong Peninsula, New Territories and surrounding small islands, with a total area of more than 1,000 square kilometers. Among the 6.78 million residents in Hong Kong, 96 per cent are Chinese. Chinese and English are used in Hong Kong.

Hong Kang has been part of the territory of China since ancient times. After the Opium War in 1840, the Qing Government ceded Hong Kong to Great Britain as a colony. Upon Hong Kang's return back to China on July 1, 1997, it was made a Special Administrative Region, and the policy of "One country, Two systems" has been successfully implemented from then on.

Hong Kong is a major center for finance, manufacturing, transporting, commerce and trade. As the Pearl of the Orient, it is also a popular tourist attraction, and is reputed as a shopper's and tourist's paradise. Recommended attractions on this wonderful area are Ocean Park, Song Dynasty Town, Victoria Park, Hong Kong Park, Hong Kong Convention and Exhibition Center, Aw Boon Haw Garden, and so on.

1 香港会议展览中心
Hong Kong Convention and Exhibition Center
2 维多利亚湾夜景
Victoria Bay at night

澳门特别行政区
MACAO SPECIAL ADMINISTRATIVE REGION

澳门被称为"东方的蒙特卡罗",博彩业具有合法性,在澳门经济中占有重要地位。旅游名胜有大三巴牌坊、葡京娱乐场、妈阁庙、国父纪念馆、东望洋山和西望洋山等。

Macao Special Administrative Region is located on the southeastern coast of China and borders Zhuhai in Guangdong Province. Covering a total area of more than 20 square kilometers, the territory of Macao comprises the Macao Peninsula, Taipa and Coloane islands. Macao's population is around 440,000 residents, of which 95 per cent is Chinese, and the rest are Portuguese and immigrants from other countries. Chinese and Portuguese are used in Macao.

Macao has been part of territory of China since ancient times. In the mid-16th century, the Portuguese occupied Macao step by step. Macao is a special administrative region of the People's Republic of China since December 20, 1999 and will maintain its social and economical characteristics in accordance to the principle of "One country, Two systems".

Known as the "Monte Carlo of the East", Macao is a famous gambling city. Gambling in Macao is legal and occupies an important position in local economy. Major attractions in Macao include St. Paul's Ruins, Casino Lisboa, A-Ma Temple, Memorial House of Dr Sun Yat-Sen, Guia Hill, and others.

澳门特别行政区位于中国东南沿海的珠江三角洲,陆路与广东省珠海市相连,由澳门半岛、凼仔岛和路环岛组成。行政区总面积20多平方公里,人口约44万,其中,95%是华人,葡萄牙人及其他外国人只占5%左右。使用中文与葡萄牙文。

澳门自古以来就是中国的领土。16世纪中叶,逐步被葡萄牙所占领。1999年12月20日,澳门回归祖国,成为中华人民共和国的一个特别行政区,依据澳门基本法,高度自治,实行"一国两制"政策。

1 大三巴牌坊
  St. Paul's Ruins
2 葡京大酒店
  Casino Lisboa
3 友谊大桥
  Friendship Bridge

香港·澳门·台湾

台湾省
TAIWAN PROVINCE

台湾省简称台。位于中国东南海面上，西隔台湾海峡与福建省相望，东濒太平洋。全省面积3.6万平方公里，是中国第一大岛，人口2000多万。台湾省地势东高西低，山地占总面积的三分之二。中部的玉山山脉主峰高3952米，为中国东南部最高峰。台湾省是美丽富饶的宝岛，主要作物有"台湾三宝"——水稻、甘蔗、茶叶，以及香蕉、菠萝、龙眼、荔枝、木瓜、橄榄等水果。

台湾自古以来就是中国的神圣领土。中国古籍中谓之为"岛夷"。隋代以前称"夷洲"。隋、唐以后至宋、元，以"流求"或"溜求"称台湾。明万历年间正式始名"台湾"。1684年，清政府在台南设台湾府；1885年，置台湾省。1895年，为日本占领。1945年抗日战争胜利后，归还中国。

台湾重要城市有台北、历史名城台南、工业港城高雄和台中等。主要风景名胜有台湾故宫博物院、日月潭、阿里山、阳明山、妈祖庙、北投温泉等。

Taiwan Province, known as *Tai* for short , is situated at China's southeast sea, facing the Pacific to the east and Fujian Province to the west across the Straits. Covering a total area of 36,000 square kilometers, it is the largest island in China and has a population of more than 20 million. The general topography is high in the east and low in the west. The general landform is extremely complicated, of which the mountainous area occupies two-thirds of the territory of the province. Yushan (Jade Mountain) in the center of Taiwan is the highest mountain in southeast China with an elevation of 3,952 meters above sea level. A beautiful and fertile land, Taiwan is extremely rich in plants. Its main crops include "Three Treasures of Taiwan" — paddy, sugar cane and tea, as well as banana, pineapple, longan, litchi, papaya, olive, and others.

Taiwan has been part of territory of China since ancient times. It was called "Daoyi" in Chinese ancient books, and "Yizhou" before the Sui Dynasty. From Sui to Yuan dynasties, it had a name of "Liuqiu". During the Emperor Wanli's reign of the Ming Dynasty, it got its present name of "Taiwan". Under the jurisdiction of Taiwan Prefecture in 1684 during the Qing Dynasty, Taiwan became a province in 1885 of the same dynasty. In 1895, Taiwan is occupied by Japan. After the winning of the War of Resistance Against Japan in 1945, Taiwan returned back to China.

Major cities in Taiwan are Taipei, Tainan, a famous historical city, Kaohsiung, an industrial harbor city and Taichung. Surrounded by sea, Taiwan's weather is agreeable and is as beautiful as a painting with bountiful tourist resources. There are such significant places of historic interest and scenic beauty as Taiwan Palace Museum, Sun and Moon Pool, Ali Mountain and Yangming Mountain scenic spots, Mazu Temple, and Beitou Hot Springs.

1　圆山大酒店
　　Grand Hotel
2　日月潭
　　Sun and Moon Pool
3　台湾故宫博物院
　　Taiwan Palace Museum

民俗风情
FOLKLORE

悠久传统的民族歌舞和少数民族的文化习俗，是中国旅游资源的一大宝库。在长期的历史发展过程中，中国各民族在饮食、服饰、居住等方面，形成了各自独特的风俗习惯和丰富多彩的民族风情，共同组成了中国绚丽多姿的民俗文化。其中，著名的民俗节庆活动有40多个，如傣族的泼水节、彝族的火把节、白族的三月街、壮族的歌圩和蒙古族的那达慕大会等；各具特色的节日则月月皆有。

Chinese music, dance and opera, and the culture and customs of ethnic minorities are treasure stores of tourism resources. During the long course of historical development, China's different peoples have devel-oped individual customs regarding food, clothing and housing, in response to their own particular environments, so-cial conditions and level of economic development. China's folklore is espe-cially gorgeous and attractive. There are more than 40 yearly famous festivals, such as the Dai Water-Sprinkling Festi-val, Yi Torch Festival, Bai March Street, Zhuang Singing Festival and Mongolian Nadam Fair. And every ethnic minority group has its own festivals.

1 蒙古族摔跤
Mongolian wrestlers
2 苗族歌舞
Miao folk dancers
3 藏族舞蹈
Tibetan dancers

4 天津文化节
Tianjin Culture Festival
5 西安仿唐乐舞
Tang-Dynasty-style dance in Xi'an, Shaanxi
6 北京中幡
Zhongfan, Beijing
7 四川成都茶馆
A view of teahouse in Chengdu, Sichuan

8 庙会舞狮表演
Lion Dance at a fair
9 云南丽江纳西族
Naxi ethnic group in Lijiang, Yunnan
10 维吾尔族叼羊
A goat-catching competition of
the Uygur nationality
11 江苏水乡妇女
Woman in a water-town in
Jiangsu
12 江苏集市
A fair view in Jiangsu
13 气功表演
Qigong performance

14 福建惠安女
   Maidens folk of Hui'an, Fujian

15 侗族节日
   A festival of Dong nationality

16 草原风情
   A festival scene on the grassland

17 云南白族妇女
   Girls of the Bai nationality

18 云南赶摆
   A festival scene of Ganbai in Yunnan

19 云南花腰傣族少女
   Girls of Flower-waist Dai, a branch of
   Dai ethnic group in Yunnan

20 傣族泼水节
   Dai's Washing-Sprinkling Festival